GREAT SCENES AND MONOLOGUES FOR CHILDREN AGES 7–14

VOLUME II

OTHER SMITH AND KRAUS BOOKS
EDITED BY CRAIG SLAIGHT AND JACK SHARRAR

Great Scenes for Young Actors, Volumes I and II

Great Monologues for Young Actors, Volumes I and II

Great Scenes and Monologues for Children, Volumes I and II

New Plays from A.C.T.'s Young Conservatory,
Volumes I, II, III, and IV

If you require prepublication information about forthcoming Smith and Kraus books, you may receive our semiannual catalogue, free of charge, by sending your name and address to *Smith and Kraus Catalogue, PO Box 127, Lyme, NH 03768*. Or call us at 1-800-895-4331. Fax: (603) 643-1831; Web site: www.SmithKraus.com.

Great Scenes
and Monologues
for Children
ages 7–14

VOLUME II

Edited by
Craig Slaight and Jack Sharrar

YOUNG ACTORS SERIES

A Smith and Kraus Book

A Smith and Kraus Book
Published by Smith and Kraus, Inc.
177 Lyme Road, Hanover, NH 03755

First Edition: April 2003
Manufactured in the United States of America
10 9 8 7 6 5 4 3 2 1

Cover and text design by Julia Gignoux, Freedom Hill Design

Library of Congress Cataloging-in-Publication Data
Great Scenes and Monologues for Children / edited by Craig Slaight
and Jack Sharrar. —1st ed.
p. cm.
Summary: Presents a collection of monologues and scenes from familiar plays and
books for young actors to perform.
ISBN 1-57525-224-4 (vol. 2)
1. Monologues—Juvenile literature. 2. Acting—Juvenile literature. [1. Monologues.
2. Acting.] I. Slaight, Craig. II. Sharrar, Jack F
PN2080.G727 1993
808.82'45—dc20   93-15723
CIP
AC

Contents

SCENES

MONOLOGUES

Introduction

Today's young people are among the brightest and most informed in all of history. They seek challenge — are hungry for challenge — but frequently they are left unchallenged, talked down to, and bombarded with media images that leave the language of the theater unexplored.

Through our work at the Young Conservatory at the American Conservatory Theater in San Francisco, we have made it our goal to discover quality dramatic literature that is challenging and age appropriate. We embrace a twofold mission: offering actor training for young people of the highest caliber and promoting and conserving fine dramatic writing with young people at its center. This mission has led us to over a decade of new play development by commissioning top professional playwrights to write new plays with a youthful perspective. Most recently, we have expanded our search for quality work through international collaborations with theater artists who share our point of view and passion. Some of the selections contained herein come from the fruits of these partnerships.

We hope that the selections in this second volume of scenes and monologues for children makes a significant contribution to those of you searching for intelligent, well-written, dramatic literature for children.

Craig Slaight and Jack Sharrar, Editors
San Francisco, California
October 2001

Looking Past Ambition

My phone rings: "This is Craig."

"Yes, I have a daughter. She's an amazing actor. She's been just astonishing ever since she was a baby. Everyone who meets her instantly asks if she's in show business. She's had classes in tap, ballet (for six years!), commercial acting, dialects, modeling (runway), résumés, makeup, and hair. She's been in the Mountain play, the Passion play, and ten community musicals. She's played Annie, Lucy, the Artful Dodger, and Joan of Arc. I know in my heart that if I could just get her an agent, she'd be the next Winona Ryder. By the way, if my kid comes and takes classes there, can she get a part in a movie?" Even when my instinct is to burst into a rousing chorus of Noel Coward's "Don't Put Your Daughter on the Stage, Mrs. Worthington," I resist. There is much of what this parent says that alarms me. As the director of the Young Conservatory at the American Conservatory Theater (A.C.T.), I attempt to look past ambition — whether it comes from the child or the well-meaning parent. If one works hard to look past ambition, one usually finds the desire to create, and in that we have the *kernel*, however deeply imbedded, of a richly human need to share. For me, it's all about sharing.

In the past fifteen years I've made training and directing young actors my art and my trade. Before that I was a professional director. It was Betty Garrett who said I should teach, subsequently Susan Stauter (now the artistic director of Secondary Education for the San Francisco Unified School District) who paved the way for me to do so, and Carey Perloff who sustains my work. Throughout these years, I've attempted to do two specific things: demystify technique and passionately demand that young people be taken seriously. To find that *kernel of the richly human need to share* in young people, you've got to take them seriously.

This isn't going to be about how to modify what we do in the professional world to make it digestible for the child. If acting is a re-creation of life experience (and for me it is), than one is capable of such re-creation whenever imagination and form allow. And if there is anything I've learned in this journey with young people in acting, it is that they have a powerful imagination and the diligence and capability to assimilate form to reveal truth.

The other thing I've learned is that young people who are interested in the arts are desirous of the most muscular and demanding training available and that they are frequently let down. If we felt that young people in the 1980s were lethargic and without vision, we are seeing anything but that in the young people of 2002. No matter where I've been (and I've worked over the last few years with young people from all over the United States and England), I've seen the same hunger in the eyes of young people everywhere.

The first look you get from a fresh crop of young actors is suspicion — it's always suspicion, with a hefty dollop of concerned expectation. Do you blame them? Let's face it, there's much to be suspicious about in this world, and often adults play into whatever the expectations are concerning young people's creative journey. The second look you get, if you've captured their attention, is a desire to explore new places in their experience — and always, always, the passion to do something well. The third look you get is the one that shows you the light behind the eye and the availability to go to a new place.

When I first started working with young people, it was the

third look that always pierced my heart. After many years directing professional actors, I felt there was something altogether different about that look of availability, and it ultimately made me make the commitment to lead them to vital actor training. I joke with Melissa Smith, the conservatory director here at A.C.T., that if you ask a graduate acting student to explore "green," you get "That's not my choice." You ask a young person to explore "green," and you get "Green? [followed by a pause of confused consternation] YEAH! Green!!!!" They're available and ready to go. In fifteen years I've not worked any differently with teenagers than I did with Julie Harris, Betty Garrett, or any professional actor. I may need to illuminate and define more, but I never need to water down, to settle for less. Where young people lack girdle-tight technique, they overwhelm in imagination and the astonishing ability to say *yes*.

So how does one answer the desirous parent or young person hell-bent on making it? I say immediately that I don't know much about making it. I offer that endless study, years of grooming, plastic surgery, coaching until you are emotionally and financially broke, engaging in countless opportunities to showcase "darling dearest," and even getting Uncle Chad to introduce you to Mel Gibson's manicurist probably won't lead to making it. I point out that for every successful boy band, there are hundreds of noisy garages overflowing with bad music, expensive equipment, and costumes, with no work in sight. But when my attempts to dissuade a young actor from studying acting with making it as his or her chief goal land on deaf ears, I next try to get at the young person's urge to share and use that kernel, that central desire, to help him or her act truthfully and dynamically.

Quite early on I realized that *what* young actors worked on was important to my work with young actors. It seemed ludicrous to dress a sixteen-year-old boy up to play Willy Lohman. Just as ludicrous was handing an intelligent, imaginative young woman the role of an animated panda bear who reveals life lessons about how to be kind by play's end. Somewhere between *Babar the Elephant* and *Death of a Salesman* there exists a voice that younger actors can approach — and they are more apt to learn techniques in character creation when the literature speaks to them. Don't get me wrong; I run screaming and kicking from indulgent, overobvious drivel that attempts to capture "teen angst." In the work at A.C.T., I've commissioned over twenty plays by major writers that look at the world through youthful eyes. When I talk with writers about this form of playwriting, I use *Romeo and Juliet* or *Antigone* as examples, and I seek the finest writers, not necessarily ones who have previously written for children. This kind of commissioned work goes far in taking young people seriously. You've never seen eyes quite as wide as the eyes of a young actor who has just been handed new pages by the playwright for the world premiere she's rehearsing.

Much like learning to speak by hearing others speak, it is crucial that we hand down the traditions of our training from one generation to the next. For me, mentors have played a large role in my learning about acting and directing. The careful hand that guided while I grew, the benevolent but stern voice that pointed to mistakes and encouraged successes, made all the difference — not only in the techniques I developed but also engendered in me a sense that I was part of an ageless tradition. This is central to the kernel. We often get caught up in the creative moment, self-absorbed in the conviction that we're creating something altogether new. For all of us, the newness is a big ingredient in the mix of our work. But people have been doing this since early cave dwellers re-created the success of the hunt over dinner (didn't they?). I find that young actors hunger for ritual and history in their work and long to be a part of something special, that same something that I longed to be a part of when I was young. When we attach more to the goal than to getting the gig, when we invest in a more richly developed continuum of experience and creativity than a shot in a Fox Network series, we begin to answer some important needs that are connected to sharing. And, more important, when young people realize the depth possible in their connection to this art form, we've done a lifelong service.

When I see late teens begin to contemplate college, conservatory, or university study, I am always a little saddened, for it is then that reality really sets in. When the young person begins to lay plans to leave the protected and nurturing environment of home, he or she starts to realize the limitations of the craft — limitations that heretofore were missing. As a child, if you wanted to act, you could act. You could find a school production, a community production, take an acting class, *create,* and there was a structure and support for the creation. When I audition a late teen, I see in his or her eyes the awareness that not everyone will get a part. More striking than this are the conversations I have in counseling sessions with my older teen actors in which they say, "But, I really want to do this. It means so much to me. There are so many people who want to do this. What if I won't be able to do this?"

And it isn't only the young people who are doing the asking. Responsible parents are equally concerned (sometimes more concerned) about the alarming statistics surrounding the profession of acting. I don't know a high school senior (or his or her parent) who has a passion to act who isn't aware of the employment statistics published yearly by Equity, SAG, and AFTRA. To these students and parents I try to encourage calm, careful planning and assure them over and over I've seen these things take care of themselves. As with a painter or a writer, if the need to act burns, one finds a way to do it. If something else comes along and becomes the flame, there shouldn't be regret. The wonderful late fiction writer William Maxwell once sent me a postcard that said, "I know it is the same in the theater as it is in fiction: just do the work and everything good will follow."

Although I've threatened, I've never actually polled the homeless who hang out around Union Square to see how many were failed actors. I try to support the passion, without apology, and at the same time counsel intelligent steps. For example, I strongly believe that in this country, a solid liberal arts education is an essential for actors. Actors need to be smart people, capable of bringing intelligence and empathy to a myriad of human experiences. It takes more than technique to illuminate a world. Having said that, I've worked with incredibly talented actors who never got a liberal arts education. Winona Ryder never attended college. Since she is one of our most illustrious alumni, should I then encourage other young actors to bypass college? Not likely. However, what seems absolutely essential — and I say this over and over — is to be *ready* when the time comes to present yourself as an actor to someone who can employ you. I stress that there may be few opportunities for such meetings and that each one will really count. Interestingly enough, this seems to land — on parents and on young people. And it is in this realization that thorough training and thorough education needs to be a given.

Too often the focus of working with young people, either in training or in the workplace, is to deliver a result as opposed to finding a process to unlock, to create, to form. Training young people to be actors needs to work in concert with helping young people develop into compassionate human beings. I've gotten so much more from the young person who understood what the character was doing, needing, feeling, struggling with than the one who, in the short time he had on a soundstage, merely performed a "bit." Young people have an uncanny way with impersonation. It often astonishes me that cliché is tolerated — even encouraged.

Often our approach with young actor training is overly concerned with the fun quotient. When will we stop encouraging the comedic improvisation games as a tool for serious actor training and begin to apply exercises that do more than entertain? I've seen too many classes that began with comedy club tactics under the guise of warm-up, only to end thirty minutes later with the expectation that the young actors were ready to work on a scene from a Tennessee Williams play. It is here that "theater games" can come into conflict with serious study, and it is the child who wants serious study who most interests me. This isn't to dismiss the pleasurable and even valuable aspects of exploring drama through recreational creation. Creation should be fun. But often I feel that when we remove obstacles in order to have fun, we trade in the opportunity for serious growth.

The cellist understands the need for drill and repetitive techniques that are often less than fun. I spent a season at the Interlochen Center for the Arts — an art center known for its high-class training in all the arts but particularly for its outstanding musical training. Those music students understood the discipline required to be an accomplished musician. It was a wonderful environment in which to teach acting. I learned so much about music training there and found that it linked with approaches to actor training more than I ever thought possible. I'm not afraid of discipline in my work with young people now. And, frankly, neither are my acting students — when once they've learned that hard work produces wondrous results. Part of taking a young person seriously is to be responsible for his or her journey — keen to make it as deep and proficient as possible. As the professional mentor in a young life we must be ready to bring passion to the work as well as discipline.

Finally, working with young actors keeps the kernel to share alive in me. It is a constant test of what I think I know and what needs to be continually reexamined. I see a mirror image of my own budding creative life in young actors, and it gives me amazing hope for the possibilities for genuine truth and beauty in our art. As we replace ourselves, we must embrace the handing on of the work with enormous generosity, consummate expectations that surpass mediocrity, and humble admiration for the birth of creation at any age. I can't think of a better way to explore my world.

Craig Slaight

Scenes

The Adventures of Huckleberry Finn
Timothy Mason (adapted from Mark Twain)

Set along the Mississippi River valley in the 1840s, here is the great American tale of Tom Sawyer's faithful, impish friend Huckleberry Finn. Young Huck escapes his Pap and the widow Douglas and sets off on classic adventures that mix suspense, mischievousness, and, most of all, a love for life that speak to young and old alike.

Two Males

In the first scene below, Huck is reunited with his friend Jim, an escaped slave. In the second scene, which immediately follows, Huck and Jim discover a dead body.

+ + +

Lights rise on bare setting, with river and riverbanks in the background. Huck enters, out of breath.

HUCK: *(Voice-over.)* In the moonlight, the river looked miles and miles across. It was late, I could tell — it *smell't* late, and everythin' was so quiet on the island, I could hear people talkin' way over to the ferry landin'. *(Huck climbs to uppermost platform and surveys the scene. He sits and stretches himself out for sleep.)* Anyways, I was pretty tired. It was goin' to be a grand mornin', with them all searchin' the river for my body, so I went right on out to sleep.
(Huck sleeps. Lights rise and the sound of birds provide transition into morning. Sound of distant cannon up the river. Huck stirs and sits up. Jim enters, but Huck doesn't

*recognize him. Huck attempts to find a vantage point to see
the stranger, approaching nearer. Jim turns around and sees
Huck. Jim is terrified; Huck is relieved.)*

HUCK: Jim! Jim — it's *you!* You sho'ly did give me a fright . . .

JIM: Don't hurt me! I never done you no harm when you was
alive, Huck Finn, and I hain't never done no harm to no
ghost . . .

HUCK: I ain't no *ghost,* dad blame it! Looky here, see for
yourself . . . *(Huck extends his arm out for Jim to touch;
he does so, tentatively.)* Go on, touch me — ain't no ghost
about me.
*(Jim takes Huck's hand, then the other. He breaks into a
big smile and hugs Huck to his chest.)*

JIM: I was powerful sorry to hear you was killed, Huck, but I
ain't no mo'. Honey, you is alive as I!

HUCK: Shore is good to see a friendly face, Jim, after all them
days stuck in Pap's shanty.
(Cannon boom.)

JIM: But look here, Huck — who *was* murdered in that shanty
if it warn't you?

HUCK: Shucks — *nobody,* Jim! I just fixed things up to look like
I was dead, so's I could get away from 'em all.
*(Huck moves upstage to look upstream at the town. Jim fol-
lows.)*

JIM: Well, yestiday night the whole town was talkin' bout you
bein' dead, and now they're all out on the river, soundin' a
cannon to make your body rise up from the bottom.

HUCK: *(With a modest grin.)* Yup. Kinder grand, ain't it.
(Cannon boom.)

HUCK: But how do *you* come to be here, Jim?
*(Jim takes off his hat and turns away from Huck, looking
out over the river.)*

JIM: Maybe I better not tell. *(Small pause.)* You wouldn't tell
on me if I was to tell you, would you, Huck?

HUCK: Blamed if I would, Jim.

JIM: *(Sitting.)* Well, it was this way. Some time after yer Pap hauled you off, there came this nigger trader from New Orleans an' he started to git mighty thick with Miz Watson. Now that Miz Watson, she treats me pretty rough, but she always said she wouldn't sell me down to New Orleans. Well, it were a lie, Huck . . .

(Cannon boom, louder.)

HUCK: *(Pulling Jim down behind the slope.)* Git down, Jim. They're gettin' closer.

(They crouch side by side, glancing out over the river as they speak in more hushed tones.)

JIM: One night I creeps to the parlor do', and the do' warn't quite shet, an' I hear Miz Watson tell the Widow she was a-goin' to sell me, 'cause she could get eight hundred dollars fo' me. The Widow, she try to git her not to do it, but I never waited to hear the res'. I hain't Miz Watson's Jim no more, Huck, I done run off.

(Cannon boom, still louder.)

HUCK: But now you're a runaway nigger, Jim! You know what that means . . .

JIM: She was a-goin' to *sell* me — away from my wife, Huck . . . away from my child'en.

HUCK: *(After a brief pause.)* You got *child'en*, Jim? You got a *fam'ly?*

JIM: Mind . . . you said you wouldn't tell.

HUCK: And I won't, Jim. People can call me a low-down Abolitionist and a slave-lover, but I said I wouldn't tell, an' I won't.

(Large cannon boom, Jim pulls Huck further down.)

JIM: There they is!

Sound of river rushing, animal calls of the night. Lights of late evening reveal the two sitting by a campfire: Jim smokes a pipe as Huck finishes his dinner.

HUCK: *(Voice-over.)* Jim an' me spent considerable time on Jackson's Island.

JIM: We cain't stay here forever, chile . . .

HUCK: *(Voice-over.)* We slept days and woke nights, topsy-turvy like.

JIM: *(Standing and stretching.)* We got to find a way down to Cairo, Illinois, Hucky.

HUCK: *(Voice-over.)* Then one night . . .

JIM: Huck, there's somethin' out there . . .

HUCK: *(He wasn't listening.)* How's that, Jim?

JIM: I say there's somethin' on the river . . . comin' this way.

HUCK: Well, what is it?

JIM: Cain't make it out, but it's mighty big.
(Huck rises and joins Jim at top of the slope.)

HUCK: *(With a small laugh, not believing his eyes.)* It almost looks like a . . . house.

JIM: Well, the river's been risin' right along . . .

HUCK: Mighta swept things off the shore . . .

JIM: That's jist what it is, Huck! It's a whole, en-tire house a-floatin' down the river!

HUCK: Wonder if they's anybody still in it . . .

JIM: Not likely, but they's bound to be some truck that there house we could use in Cairo. I's goin' aboard . . .
(Jim runs down to stage level; Huck follows.)

HUCK: So'm I!

JIM: No, you ain't, chile. Din't you see how sprightly that thing is movin'? I'm goin' aboard; you stan' by.

HUCK: Stand by for what?

JIM: Blamed if I know — jist stan' by. Look now . . . here she come . . . *(Jim runs off stage left.)*

HUCK: (Calling.) Jim! Don't you be too long on that house. (Music. Vague shapes and shadows appear off stage right; sound of rushing water has increased. Huck observes for a bit, then calls again.)

HUCK: Jim?

(No answer.)

HUCK: It's movin' too fast, Jim. Come on back!

(Pause. Suddenly a call.)

JIM: Huck! Here it come — now you catch it!

(A bundle is hurled onto the shore upstage right. Huck picks it up.)

HUCK: That's good, Jim — now come on off that thing!

(The house has approached upstage center.)

JIM: They's a white man a-sleepin' in here!

HUCK: A white man? He'll make trouble for you , Jim . . .

JIM: Well, we cain't leave him lie!

HUCK: I know we cain't but . . . Jim? Jim!

(The house is moving off stage right.)

HUCK: You slippin' away, Jim! (Pause.) Jim? (Another pause. Quieter.) Jim . . . (Huck sinks to his knees, nearly in tears. Long pause and music fades out. Finally Jim appears, wet and dripping, from stage right; he carries a bundle.)

JIM: Hucky?

HUCK: (Whirling around.) Jim!

(Jim drops the bundle and Huck runs to him, then stops himself from embracing Jim.)

JIM: (Tousling Huck's hair and laughing.) You warn't worried 'bout ol' Jim, was you, Honey?

HUCK: Nope. (He wipes his eyes.) What about the man?

JIM: (Slight pause.) He warn't sleepin'. He were dead. Shot in the back.

HUCK: Jiminy! Who was it, you reckon?

(A sound of creaking boards and rushing water. Jim and Huck turn their heads upstage right at the sound.)

JIM: Look, Hucky! She's goin' down! She's sinkin'!

HUCK: Bless my soul . . .

(A huge rush of water, and then nothing but the quiet passage of the river. Jim shakes his head and turns back to center stage and the bundles.)

HUCK: I wonder who that man was . . .

JIM: Bad luck, talkin' 'bout the dead.

HUCK: . . . wonder who shot him . . . an' what for . . .

JIM: *(Angry.)* Talk like that'll fetch nothin' but bad luck, you min' my words! *(Pause.)* Looky here. Huck — a lantern for us. An' a bran'-new Barlow knife . . .

HUCK: *(Immediately interested, joining Jim in the rummaging.)* A Barlow knife?! Why, that's wuth two bits in any store . . . you call that bad luck?

JIM: An' a couple o' ol', dirty calico dresses . . .

HUCK: An' a bonnet . . . *(Huck puts the bonnet on his head.)* How d' I look, Jim?

JIM: *(Laughs.)* An ol' book . . . an' here's a fine blanket . . . Huck, there's somethin' sewn into the linin' . . . right here . . . *(Jim uses the knife on the blanket and silver dollars fall out.)* Huck!

HUCK: Eight dollars silver! Bad *luck?!* Now what did you say, day before yestiday, when I fetched in that snakeskin I found on top o' the ridge?

JIM: I said it was the wust luck in the world to touch a snakeskin — worse'n lookin' at the moon over your left shoulder — and it *is.*

HUCK: Well, here's your bad luck: We've raked in all this truck an' eight dollars besides!

JIM: *(Walking away from him.)* Don't you get too pert, Honey . . . it's a-comin'. Mind you, the bad luck's a-comin'! *(Pause.)*

HUCK: Hey, Jim — don't you wish you knew what was goin' on over to town?

JIM: I'd like to know if Miz Watson's done put a reward out on me . . .

HUCK: How's if I take the canoe an' slip over tomorrow?
(Slight pause as Jim considers.)

JIM: Well, you'll have to go in the dark and look sharp . . . Say, Hucky — that bonnet don't look half-bad on you. You git yo'self into one o' them calico dresses, an' won't nobody know you's Huck Finn.

HUCK: Hey, Jim, that *is* good. *(Huck holds one of the dresses to himself.)* Huck Finn? My name's . . . Sarah.
(Jim laughs.)

HUCK: Sarah Williams to you, Jim.
(Jim's laugh grows as lights fade to blackout.)

Afternoon of the Elves
Y York (adapted from Janet Taylor Lisle)

Based on Janet Taylor Lisle's award-winning book, fourth-grader Hillary Lenox is befriended by two neighbor girls, who teach her how to "fit in." But Sara Kate, the outcast little girl next door, draws Hillary to her with the discovery of a secret elf village in the backyard.

Two Females

In the first scene, Hillary enters Sara Kate's backyard, drawn by her curiosity of the elf village. In the second scene, Hillary, growing more skeptical, questions Sara Kate further about the "elf" people in the backyard.

Sara Kate's backyard. This yard is the antithesis of the Lenox yard. There are old appliances, car engines, tires, brambles. There, in the midst of the mess, is an orderly elf village. Little houses built with sticks, string, rocks, and leaves; separated by rows of rocks into an elf development. A well in the center of "town." Sara Kate is working on the elf village. Hillary enters with her book bag through the hedge; without looking at Hillary, Sara Kate speaks.

SARA KATE: I first saw it a couple of days ago, it just sort of appeared. They must work all through the night, but it isn't done. You can see where a couple of houses aren't finished, and there's places made ready for houses with no houses on them yet.

HILLARY: How did you know I was here?

SARA KATE: Do you want to see the village or not?

HILLARY: OK. *(Impressed.)* Wow. Too-too good. Look, they used sticks and leaves for roofs. And rocks to separate the little houses. It's a little neighborhood.

SARA KATE: Yeah, they took rocks from our driveway.

HILLARY: They stole them?

SARA KATE: Yeah, there's rocks gone from our driveway.

HILLARY: Should we put them back?

SARA KATE: No, the elves *need* them, and we don't even *have* a car anymore.

HILLARY: You don't have a *car?*

SARA KATE: No. So what?

HILLARY: Nothing. *(Beat.)* Well, they shouldn't steal. Even rocks.

SARA KATE: The elves don't think so.

HILLARY: *(Shocked.)* They don't think it's wrong to steal?

SARA KATE: Elves have different rules.

HILLARY: They *steal?!*

SARA KATE: Just stuff nobody is using. Or stuff from mean rich people.

HILLARY: How do they know who's mean?

SARA KATE: They just know.

HILLARY: Look, a well, a tiny little well. Let's haul up some water.

SARA KATE: Leave it alone. It's very fragile.

HILLARY: It *all* looks real fragile. What happens when it rains?

SARA KATE: They rebuild and repair. Elves are at the complete mercy of earth forces.

HILLARY: *(Pause.)* How do you know so much?

SARA KATE: . . . I think the elves sneak stuff into my brain.

HILLARY: What do you mean?

SARA KATE: I tried to haul up some water and all of a sudden I was thinking "the elves won't like this."

HILLARY: *(Beat.)* Sara Kate, are you sure elves built this? Maybe this was built by mice. Mice could live in these houses quite nicely.

SARA KATE: Mice! That is really — that is just — that is so *stupid!* When did you ever hear of mice building houses?!

HILLARY: Or even a person could have built these houses.

SARA KATE: Look, I didn't have to invite you here today, and I didn't have to show you this. I thought you might like to see an elf village for a change. If you don't believe elves built this, that's your problem. I *know* they did.

HILLARY: I never saw elves in *my* backyard.

SARA KATE: Well, of course not.

HILLARY: What do you mean?

SARA KATE: *(Sincere, kind.)* Elves would never go in your backyard, no offense, Hillary, but your backyard would not offer any protection. See, elves need to hide, they hate it when people see them. In the olden days, it didn't matter so much, but now, there's too many people, and too many bad ones; elves can't risk being seen by a bad person.

HILLARY: *(Worried.)* Why? What would happen?

SARA KATE: There's no telling, but it would be very terrible. They know they're safe here, there's a million places to hide in this yard.

HILLARY: *(Looks around, impressed.)* Yeah, I see what you mean.

(Hillary sneaks up on things and peeks behind them, looking for elves, as she begins to believe Sara Kate's elf information.)

SARA KATE: Where, for example, would they find stones in your yard to make these little private lots?

HILLARY: *(Realization.)* Right. Our driveway is all paved with cement. There's no rocks anywhere in our yard. And Dad rakes the leaves the second they fall; so there's nothing to make a roof out of! *(She begins to skip.)* Wow. Your yard is perfect for elves! Look at all the junk to hide in, and strings and wire to make the houses, and rocks, and leaves for roofs. *(She stops skipping abruptly.)* Oh, is it all right to skip?

SARA KATE: What are you talking about? *(Sara Kate skips and jumps and prances about.)* Of course it's all right to skip. It makes the elves really happy.

HILLARY: It does? *(She skips.)*

SARA KATE: Yes! And if you make them happy enough, they trust you and let you peek at them. *(Stops suddenly.)* Listen! I hear them laughing now.

(Hillary stops skipping. They listen.)

SARA KATE: Their language is like earth sounds. But if you listen real careful, you can hear that it's really elves.

(Both girls are affected by a felt presence. Hillary is amazed.)

HILLARY: *(Whispers.)* Sara Kate? I think they're here.

SARA KATE: Yes, I feel it too. Don't talk about them or they'll go away. Act natural.

(Hillary tries to act natural. She hums and opens her book bag.)

SARA KATE: *(Disdain.)* Are you doing *homework?!*

HILLARY: *(Whispers.)* I was going to write something down. In my diary.

SARA KATE: Don't whisper, whispering isn't natural. What are you going to write?

HILLARY: About the elves. I keep a record, a written record of everything. I document my life.

SARA KATE: Why do you want to do that?

HILLARY: In case we get famous — me and Alison and Jane. I have all our documentation in our diary.

SARA KATE: I don't want to be famous. *(Beat.)* I'm going to straighten the rocks.

HILLARY: I can do that, too.

SARA KATE: I don't want to interrupt your documenting.

HILLARY: It's no interruption.

(Hillary puts diary in book bag. The girls start to straighten rocks at one of the "lots.")

HILLARY: Oh, look.

SARA KATE: Little steps.

HILLARY: *(At the same time.)* Little steps!

SARA KATE: Oh! Orion's belt, the Big Dipper, the Little Dipper, the Pleiades, Virgo, Gemini, Aquarius, Libra, Pisces, Capricorn. Ten! *(Beat.)* How come you didn't punch me?

HILLARY: What are you talking about?!

SARA KATE: Ten stars. We said the same thing at the same time. You're supposed to punch me while I say ten stars.

HILLARY: *(Realizing.)* Sara Kate, you're supposed to say "pididdle," and then make *me* say ten of something, and punch *me*. You don't have it right at all.

SARA KATE: *(Flares up.)* Who cares?! It's *your* stupid game. I just did it because I thought *you* liked it, *I* don't like it, it's a stupid game. Who cares?!

HILLARY: *(Trying to end the argument.)* I'm sorry, I didn't mean — you're right! It *is* a stupid game, you're right. Who cares?

SARA KATE: Yeah, who cares.

(Pause. Hillary walks near the elf houses.)

HILLARY: *(An idea.)* The elves must think we're giants!

SARA KATE: *(Impressed.)* What?!

HILLARY: Yes! They think we are kindly human giants! *(Stands on something to look around.)* Kindly giant sisters who watch over elves.

SARA KATE: *(Pretending to keep watch, a giant voice.)* The kindly giant sisters scan the horizon for signs of danger! All clear on the western bank!

HILLARY: *(Playing along.)* All clear on the eastern bank.

(Hillary walks in a large fashion. A lumbering, giant walk. Sara Kate does too.)

HILLARY: The kindly giant sisters walk the land, keeping watch.

SARA KATE: The ground quakes with their steps.

HILLARY: But the elves have no fear.

(A figure appears in a window. It is a thin woman wearing a nightgown; she is clearly very ill, with wild hair.)

SARA KATE: No dangerous humans in sight.

HILLARY: Only the kindly *giant sisters.*

SARA KATE: *(At the same time.)* — *Giant sisters.* All elves must proceed to their homes.

(Hillary sees the figure in the window. She is frozen in fear.)

SARA KATE: Elves may continue construction on the village. The kindly giant sisters will lift and carry objects of great size — *(Sara Kate notices Hillary and looks to the house where she sees the figure.)*

SARA KATE: You have to go.

HILLARY: What is — who is —

SARA KATE: Just go. You have to go.

HILLARY: But I —

SARA KATE: No buts. Get going.

HILLARY: But you shouldn't —

SARA KATE: Here! Here's your bag. Just take it and go. Go home, Hillary.

(Hillary leaves through the hedge. Sara Kate sighs and turns toward the house, where the figure has disappeared.)

✦ ✦ ✦

The Connolly backyard. Sara Kate. An elf-sized Ferris wheel made from bicycle tire rims, quite amazing. There are other changes as well. Hillary, carrying her old jacket and book bag, comes quietly through the hedge; Sara Kate couldn't possibly hear.

SARA KATE: Isn't it beautiful?

HILLARY: I didn't make a sound; how did you know I was here?

SARA KATE: I don't *know*; I just . . . know. *(About the wheel.)* What do you think?

HILLARY: *(She drops her jacket and book bag and walks around and admires it.)* It's really something. Tiny little seats.

SARA KATE: Elf size.

HILLARY: How did they carry the tires?

SARA KATE: Many many of them working together.

HILLARY: How do you know?

SARA KATE: Information gets into my brain.

HILLARY: Is it a voice gets in your brain?

SARA KATE: Yes.

HILLARY: What's it sound like?

SARA KATE: It sounds . . . like me. *(Beat.)* The tires are from that old bike. See? The bike tires are gone. These are those tires.

HILLARY: How are you going to ride it?

SARA KATE: It's an old piece of junk; nobody could ride it. See this?

(Something that might be a tiny swimming pool.)

HILLARY: A swimming pool. Oh my goodness! They made a little swimming pool.

SARA KATE: Or something.

HILLARY: You know what? I bet they're going to make a whole amusement park. Right in your backyard. Merry-go-round, roller coaster. It's perfect. The elves will ride the rides until they get hot, and then they'll go for a swim.

SARA KATE: *(Unconvinced.)* Maybe.

HILLARY: What do you mean "maybe"?

SARA KATE: Elves are not tiny human beings. They're elves, completely different from humans. It's possible to jump to wrong conclusions.

(Hillary considers the pool.)

HILLARY: *(An idea.)* It's a power source.

SARA KATE: *(Impressed.)* Aaaah, yessss; combination hydro and photovoltaics.

HILLARY: Yeah, a power source.

SARA KATE: *(Playing.)* The power streams down from the sun —

HILLARY: *(Playing.)* And the stars, too. It never stops coming down, a never-ending source of power —

SARA KATE: If you're feeling a little energy drain, stop at the power pool —

HILLARY: For a fill-up. *(Sticks her finger in the pool; she expands.)* I'm filling up with power. Pow, pow.

SARA KATE: Don't explode!

HILLARY: Now I'm full of energy. Energy to heat the houses.

SARA KATE: Except elves don't get cold.

HILLARY: No way!

SARA KATE: Well, they dooooo, but not until it's freezing. When they finally get so cold they can't stand it, they move into empty human houses. *(Neatens the village.)* Come on, the kindly giant sisters must help the elves again.

HILLARY: The Hillary giant lines up the scattered stones around the elf houses.

SARA KATE: The Sara Kate giant gathers berries for the elves' dinner.

HILLARY: And the Hillary giant helps her.

(Sara Kate eats berries. Hillary sees and tries some; they're terrible.)

HILLARY: Yuk. These are terrible, yuk. Poison I bet.

SARA KATE: *(Playing.)* Not to an elf. *(Pops a berry in her mouth.)*

HILLARY: *(Serious.)* Don't eat that, Sara Kate. *(Beat.)* Are you hungry?

SARA KATE: *(Serious.)* I'm not hungry.

HILLARY: You can eat at my house.

SARA KATE: *(Subdued.)* No. I eat with my mom. *(The game again.)* Here. Put leaves and little sticks in this box, Hillary giant.

(Sara Kate suddenly turns, as if to see something. Hillary looks, too, but the elves are gone.)

SARA KATE: Gone.

HILLARY: I wish I could see an elf.

SARA KATE: You have to sort of see them out of the corner of your eye.

(Hillary looks forward, trying to see sideways.)

SARA KATE: Don't worry if you don't see one right away. It might take them a long time to trust us. Move your bag.

(Hillary picks up her book bag, remembers her diary. Starts looking around.)

HILLARY: If the elves took the tires and all, but they need them to cool off and stuff, I think that's all right.

SARA KATE: *(Not really paying attention, walking in the giant way.)* Of course, it's all right.

HILLARY: But it would probably be wrong if they took some-body's personal stuff.

SARA KATE: Human rules don't work for elves. What are you doing way over there?

HILLARY: If there was something that a human being *owned* and *needed* and *loved,* and an elf didn't need it or love it or any-thing. It would be wrong for that elf to take it.

SARA KATE: What are you *doing?* There's no building materials over there.

HILLARY: I'm looking for something.

SARA KATE: What?

HILLARY: My diary. I'm looking for my diary.

SARA KATE: Your diary isn't over there.

HILLARY: *(Hopeful.)* Where is it?

SARA KATE: How should I know? Is that what this is about? Your diary? *(Beat.)* You *do* think I stole your diary.

HILLARY: *(Too fast.)* No. No. I . . . I lost it. I can't find it. And I had it here yesterday, so I thought, maybe.

SARA KATE: What?! You thought, what?!

HILLARY: I thought . . . maybe . . . I *left* it here. By mistake.

SARA KATE: You think I sneaked into your stupid book bag and stole your stupid diary. Boy, you *are* the same as Jane and Alison. Every time something happens, you blame it on me. You are sickening.

HILLARY: *(Getting mad.)* What am I supposed to think? The last time I ever saw it I was here —

SARA KATE: *(Shouting.)* Who cares what you think? You're a stupid little girl with stupid little friends.

HILLARY: *(Shouting.)* I am not stupid and my friends are not stupid. We have a song —

SARA KATE: A stupid song to show how stupid your brains are —

HILLARY: Don't you call us stupid. You got held back. You're the only one's stupid around here.

SARA KATE: Get out. Get out of my yard.

HILLARY: I was going to give you my jacket. I brought my jacket all the way over here to give it to you.

SARA KATE: Who wants your stupid jacket?! Get out.

(The Ferris wheel spins by itself, whirs, dazzles. The girls are silent, amazed. Hillary stops it.)

SARA KATE: *(Gently.)* Why did you stop it?

HILLARY: It scared me.

SARA KATE: *(Sympathizing.)* Oh, don't be scared of elves. Elves can't hurt people. People can hurt elves is all.

(The window shade on the house is pulled to one side.)

HILLARY: Do you want my jacket? My mother said I could give it to you. I got this new one.

SARA KATE: So you could match your good friends.

HILLARY: . . . You never wear a coat.

SARA KATE: I don't . . . get cold.

HILLARY: Like an elf.

(Sara Kate notices the window shade.)

SARA KATE: Oh, man. I gotta go before the bank closes. Do you want to go shop with me?

HILLARY: Do you go to the corner, to Mr. Neal's?

SARA KATE: No. I go to the supermarket. Things are cheaper, and it's . . . just better to go to the big stores.

HILLARY: My mother would kill me if I went all the way to the supermarket.

SARA KATE: So don't go, no skin off my nose.

HILLARY: No, OK, I'll go. I'll go with you.

Anne of Green Gables

R. N. Sandberg (adapted from L. M. Montgomery)

Anne of Green Gables is a faithful adaptation of L. M. Montgomery's classic tale of the same name. Telling the story of Anne, the high-spirited little girl who captures the hearts of everyone in the quaint village of Avonlea, this play unlocks the hearts of all.

Two Females

In the first scene, Anne speaks to her friend Diana of the wonderful places she imagines. The scene that follows finds Anne and Diana playing at "ladies having tea." In the third scene, Anne and Diana are headed for a picnic in a small boat.

✦ ✦ ✦

The woods.

ANNE: Oh, just smell the pine, here. Can't you imagine fairies dancing on the smell as if it were a magic carpet?

DIANA: Not really.

ANNE: I don't know how people live without flowers and trees. I expect people in desolate climates must be extremely depressed all the time. They've nothing lovely to look at or smell.

DIANA: Perhaps, they don't notice. They've never seen them, so they don't miss them.

ANNE: I've imagined all kinds of lovely places even though I've never seen them.

DIANA: Really? I never imagine anything. *(An awkward pause.)* I think we should be getting back.

ANNE: Would you like a shortbread?

DIANA: It's starting to get dark.

ANNE: Just one, then we'll go. They're very good. Marilla uses extra butter.

DIANA: All right.

ANNE: Marilla's an excellent cook. I even like her vegetables.

DIANA: These are delicious. Like something the Queen might eat. Can I have another?

ANNE: *(Handing her one.)* Do you really never imagine things?

DIANA: I haven't the knack for it.

ANNE: But you said these were the kind of thing the Queen might eat.

DIANA: That's not real imagining.

ANNE: You mean like fantastic wizards and terrible monsters?

DIANA: Yes.

ANNE: Don't you ever imagine that things are different in your life? Your mother, for instance?

DIANA: I suppose. But that really doesn't take much imagination. *(They look at each other and laugh.)*

ANNE: It can be fun, sometimes, to imagine from real life. Like these woods. Imagine what happens here at the very dead of night.

DIANA: We should go before the light's completely gone.

ANNE: I expect it's pitch black, then. The kind of place that ghosts might choose for their revelry. The way those branches hang down. They seem to be moving even though there's not a breath of wind.

DIANA: Let's go, shall we?

ANNE: Don't you think a haunted wood is very romantic?

DIANA: This wood isn't haunted.

ANNE: You do believe in ghosts, don't you?

DIANA: Charlie Sloane says that his grandmother saw his grandfather driving home the cows one night after he'd been buried a year.

ANNE: So there could be ghosts here. Look at the way that tree's swaying. It's as if a lady's walking slowly along the bank, nodding her head, wringing her hands, uttering wailing cries. Listen. Do you hear it?

DIANA: Yes.

ANNE: Soft, wailing cries. There's a death in her family. A little murdered child.

DIANA: Oh!

ANNE: There's a light gleaming between the boughs. It's a skeleton.

DIANA: A headless horseman!

ANNE: Do you feel it?

DIANA: What?

ANNE: Something cold on your neck.

DIANA: Yes.

ANNE: Like icy fingers creeping slowly around, slowly around.

DIANA: They're going to squeeze!

(They scream. They run off and collapse on the ground. They look at each other and burst out laughing together.)

DIANA: That was wonderful.

ANNE: You can imagine, you see.

DIANA: I'm glad you've come to Green Gables.

ANNE: Do you think, Diana — do you think you can like me a little — enough, perhaps, to be my bosom friend?

DIANA: Why, I guess so. It will be jolly to have a friend. There isn't any other girl who lives very near, and my sister's such a little bitty thing.

ANNE: Will you swear to be my friend for ever and ever?

DIANA: I don't mind.

ANNE: We must join hands — so. I'll recite the oath first. I solemnly swear to be faithful to my bosom friend, Diana Barry, as long as the sun and the moon shall endure. Now you say it and put my name in.

DIANA: I solemnly swear to be faithful to my bosom friend, Anne (with an "e") Shirley, as long as the sun and the moon shall endure.

(Anne turns away.)

DIANA: Anne?

ANNE: *(Wiping away a tear.)* It's nothing.

DIANA: *(Hesitates, then.)* It's a raindrop.

ANNE: Yes. A salty raindrop.

DIANA: An ocean raindrop.

ANNE: A flood of them.

DIANA: An ocean of rain.

ANNE: A ferocious storm about to overwhelm us.

DIANA: We'd better run.

ANNE: Yes, run. Run for the palace.

DIANA: Run for home.

(They run off, laughing.)

✦ ✦ ✦

The dining room. Anne and Diana, who is quite dressed up, enter. They are playing at "ladies having tea."

ANNE: Won't you please come in.

DIANA: Why thank you.

ANNE: Won't you please sit down.

DIANA: Why thank you.

ANNE: I greatly enjoyed our stroll round your lovely Lake of the Shining Waters, this afternoon.

DIANA: Why thank you. I know I shall enjoy your hospitality greatly.

ANNE: Why thank *you!* Oh, this is such fun, isn't it, Diana? Do you know what Marilla said we could have for tea? Fruit-cake, cherry preserves, and raspberry cordial!

DIANA: I love raspberry cordial!

ANNE: Well, then, my dear, may I serve you a glass?

DIANA: I'd be ever so grateful.

ANNE: I shall bring it directly. *(Anne goes to the cabinet.)* Marilla said it was right here.

DIANA: It's been so awful without you at school, Anne. You've missed ever so much. Ruby Gillis charmed her warts away with a magic pebble that she got from old Mary Jo.

ANNE: Here it is, I believe. *(She gets the bottle from the hutch and brings it to the table.)*

DIANA: Charlie Sloane's name was written with Em White's on the porch wall; she was real mad about it. And Gilbert Blythe did the most awful thing to Tillie Boulter . . .

ANNE: *(Interrupts her.)* Please, Diana.

DIANA: You're really being silly, Anne.

ANNE: I shall never forgive Gilbert Blythe.

DIANA: He's truly sorry.

ANNE: Let's not spoil our one afternoon together. *(She hands Diana a glass of cordial.)*

DIANA: All right.

ANNE: I'll get the tea. *(She starts off.)*

DIANA: *(Sipping daintily.)* This is awfully nice raspberry cordial, Anne.

ANNE: *(Off.)* I'm real glad you like it. Take as much as you want.

DIANA: *(Takes a very large drink.)* Mmm, the nicest I ever drank. *(She drains the glass and pours herself another.)* This raspberry cordial is ever so much nicer than Mrs. Lynde's although she brags of hers so much. *(She drinks most of the glass down.)* It doesn't taste a bit like Mrs. Lynde's. *(Drinks.)*

ANNE: *(Re-entering.)* I should think Marilla's would prob'ly be much nicer than Mrs. Lynde's. Marilla is a famous cook. Will you have some more?

DIANA: Thank you.

(As Anne talks, she pours Diana's drink, then proceeds to make and pour the tea and cut and serve the cake and pre-

serves. While Anne talks and does all this, the cordial has begun to affect Diana: she gradually becomes quite woozy and ill. Anne, who is involved with her story and tasks, does not really notice Diana's illness.)

ANNE: Marilla's trying to teach me to cook, but it's uphill work. There's so little scope for imagination in cookery. You have to go by rules. The last time I made a cake I forgot to put the flour in. I was imagining a lovely story about you and me. You had smallpox and I was nursing you back to health. The cake was a dismal failure. Flour is so essential to cakes, you know. Marilla was very cross, and I don't blame her. I'm a trial to her. Last week, Marilla made a pudding sauce to serve to Mr. and Mrs. Chester Ross. She told me to put it on the shelf and cover it, but when I was carrying it I was imagining I was a nun taking the veil to bury a broken heart and I forgot about covering the sauce. When I finally remembered to cover it, I found a mouse drowned in it. I took the mouse out, of course, but Marilla was milking at the time and I forgot to tell her until I saw her carrying the sauce to the table. I screamed, "Marilla, you mustn't use that pudding sauce. There was a mouse drowned in it, and I forgot to tell you." Marilla and Matthew and Mr. and Mrs. Ross all just stared at me.

DIANA: I — I — don't feel so well. I — need to go home.

ANNE: You mustn't dream of going home. You haven't had your tea.

DIANA: I've got to go home.

ANNE: What about your cake and preserves?

(Diana groans.)

ANNE: Lie down for a little and you'll feel better. Where do you feel bad?

DIANA: I'm — I'm awful sick.

ANNE: Oh, Diana, do you suppose you really are taking the

smallpox? If you are, I'll never forsake you. But I do wish you'd stay till after tea.

DIANA: *(Getting up.)* I'm dizzy. *(She falls.)*

ANNE: Diana!

✦ ✦ ✦

On the bank of the river. Anne and Diana are in a small boat in the water. Diana is happily rowing. Anne is slightly nervous. They wear heavy coats.

DIANA: This is ever so much fun, isn't it Anne?

ANNE: Yes. But I do wish I knew how to swim.

DIANA: This tub may be old as the dawn, but I don't think it's in danger of sinking, just yet.

ANNE: There's an awful lot of water seeping in. Oh, it's cold.

DIANA: Yes, a body wouldn't last five minutes in the water. Not quite the ideal for a picnic. But end of term deserves some kind of celebration.

(Diana pops out of the boat and pulls it on the bank. Anne, who climbs out quickly, holds a picnic basket.)

ANNE: One more week.

DIANA: Yes, you'll know on Friday whether you've beaten Gilbert or not.

ANNE: What's important is we're together again.

DIANA: If you win top scholar will you forgive him?

ANNE: I don't want to discuss it.

DIANA: Think how you felt when my mother wouldn't forgive you.

ANNE: I don't care how he feels.

DIANA: You expect everyone to care about how you feel.

ANNE: Oh we're in luck. Hot cocoa and Marilla's special muffins.

DIANA: He's apologized. He's never teased you again. In fact, he's been overly nice to you. What does he have to do, Anne?

ANNE: He's just so arrogant.

DIANA: He's sure of himself, that's all. No reason he shouldn't be. He's always been top.

ANNE: Well, he won't be this year. I've mastered geometry and all that's left is the recitation. I'm going to make sure mine is so powerful that no one will have any doubt who is the winner. I'm going to recite "The Lady of Shallot."

DIANA: Oh, that's so romantic! Floating down the river to Camelot, drawn by Lancelot from her seclusion to her death. You'll be wonderful, Anne.

ANNE: I shall be more than wonderful. I shall become the Lady of Shallot. When I finish, everyone will have seen that awful combination of death and beauty reflected right on my face.

DIANA: Oh, that's ghastly! How will you do it?

ANNE: *(Pauses, then looks towards the boat.)* I shall experience her pain, firsthand. Come on. *(She goes to the boat.)*

DIANA: What are you going to do?

ANNE: *(Taking off her coat.)* Down she came and found a boat.

DIANA: Anne!

(Anne takes the paddle out of the boat.)

ANNE: Beneath a willow left afloat,

And round about the prow she wrote — *(Looks at Diana.)*

DIANA: The Lady of Shallot.

ANNE: *(From in the boat.)* Well, push me off.

DIANA: Into the river?

ANNE: Yes.

DIANA: No!

ANNE: Diana, I've got to float down the river, singing my mournful, holy song.

DIANA: And dying!

ANNE: *(Getting up.)* All right, I'll push myself off. I thought as my bosom friend you'd want to be part of this. This is entering the world of Camelot, of Lancelot, of —

DIANA: The Lady of Shallot.

ANNE: Yes.

DIANA: All right. Lie back down.

(Anne does. She walks slowly toward the boat, starts to undo the rope from shore.)

DIANA: Lying robed in snowy white.

That loosely flew to left and right —

DIANA: The leaves upon her falling light

Thro' the noises of the night —

Beauty and the Beast
Constance Congdon

In this adaptation of the popular children's tale, Belle, a happy and giving young girl, must care for her quarrelsome siblings. When her father is stranded in a foreign land and taken into the castle of an ominous beast, Belle goes to the beast, against her father's wishes, to seek his release. In time, Belle learns to love the beast and becomes more self-reliant.

One Male and One Female (and two nonspeaking parts)

Belle is in the rose garden attending to the rose beds, with the help of one of her attendants, Minion (a monkey), when the Beast, who is falling under Belle's charm, enters.

Belle is in the rose garden. She seems at home there and is working very hard, gardening in bare feet. Minion serves as helper, standing near like a butler, holding a silver platter with gardening tools and Belle's fine slippers. Belle and Minion are wearing smocks over fine garments — smocks made of something serviceable such as sheets from Belle's room that Belle adapted into smocks. Skirt of Belle's gown is tucked up to keep it from getting dirty.

BELLE: These beds need so much work — all these lovely roses getting root bound, it's a shame. Roses are a flower that give back double in beauty what they get in care. *(Pruning rose hips.)* Now, these are rose hips, Gabrielle. Save those, and we'll make tea with them, or if we gather enough, jelly. *(Minion puts rose hips on silver platter.)*

I hope I'm not getting dirty. I put on these beautiful gowns every day because there's nothing else to wear. You haven't found my old clothes, have you?

(Minion shakes its head no.)

You and Suzanne were the last to see them.

(Minion shrugs.)

My shoes? I refuse to wear those fine slippers for every day — it's immoral.

(Minion offers Belle her slippers.)

After I've washed my feet.

(Other Minion enters hurriedly.)

What is it? What's wrong?

(Shadow appears, then Beast enters. Minions bow, very afraid of Beast's anger about being "out of uniform.")

BEAST: *(To Minion in smock.)* What . . . do . . . you . . . wear . . . in . . . my . . . castle?!

(Minion scrambles to take smock off, drops tray in doing so.)

BELLE: *(To Beast.)* Stop it! *(To Minion.)* Gabrielle, come here.

(Minions exit. Belle stoops to pick up mess. Beast stops her.)

BEAST: Don't . . . touch that. . . . They . . . will . . . do . . . it.

BELLE: When work needs to be done, do it! That is the way to live in the world. But what would you know about that? You're not part of the world!

BEAST: I . . . want . . . to . . . be . . . again. So let me. *(Cleans up mess and stands.)* Sorry to have bothered you. *(Starts to exit.)*

BELLE: Beast, don't leave! You're always leaving. You sit at dinner with me and never eat a bite yourself. And then ask me that . . . question, and I answer no, and then you leave me! I don't know how many weeks I've been here, but it's always the same. Now, come back, please. And stay. I . . . need the company.

(Beast comes back.)

BELLE: Could we just sit? And talk?

BEAST: Sit . . . Good. *(An order to absent Minion.)* Sit!!!
(Minions, without smocks, enter with chairs and set them down. Beast motions for them to leave.)

BELLE: Oh, let them stay. They are my only friends. Come on, Gabrielle. Come on, Suzanne. Beast will let you stay.
(Minion helps Belle out of smock and takes it.)

BEAST: "Gabrielle"? . . . "Suzanne"?

BELLE: Oh, I named them Gabrielle and Suzanne, after my sisters.

BEAST: *(Pointing at Minions.)* "Gabrielle"? "Suzanne"?
(Beast laughs. Minions, having never seen this reaction from Beast, are completely amazed, confused, and alarmed. After beat, they try to administer to him as if he were having attack of heat prostration.)
Oh, that felt good . . . Belle, perhaps you've already begun to . . . save my life.
(Beast takes Belle's hand and kisses it.) Garden is . . . beautiful! Sing, roses!
(Roses sing to Belle. Minions dance; Belle joins them.)

BELLE: It feels so good to dance. It's been so very long. Even at home I never danced, I was always too busy working.
(Dances beat or two more.) Can you dance, Beast?

BEAST: No!

BELLE: Try.

BEAST: *No.*

BELLE: Why, you're frightened. What are you afraid of, Beast?

BEAST: Your laughter.

BELLE: Why do you think I would laugh at you?

BEAST: Beautiful ones always laugh at ugliness.

BELLE: Well, then they're not really beautiful, are they! Besides, you're not ugly — where did you get that idea?

BEAST: From your eyes.
(Beat.)

BELLE: Here. Take my hand. *(She gets him to dance.)* See? Not difficult.

BEAST: I knew a dance once.

(He does some dance step with her — some remnant from his life as human being. Suddenly, Belle steps on rock and hurts foot.)

BELLE: Ow!

BEAST: Belle! *(Beast swoops her up in his arms quickly to protect her.)* What was it?

BELLE: Just a rock.

BEAST: Is Belle all right?

BELLE: I'm fine. Really.

BEAST: Where are your shoes?

(To Minions.)

Shoes!

BELLE: Put me down, Beast. I'm fine.

BEAST: Must I?

BELLE: Yes.

(Beast puts her down in chair. Minion brings Belle's slippers.)

BELLE: No, I won't put those on until I wash my feet — I told you.

(Minion enters with basin of water and towel, ready to wash Belle's feet. Beast kneels before Belle in chair, and she thinks he's going to propose.)

BELLE: Don't ask me that question today, Beast. We're having such a good time.

BEAST: *(Holding up and looking at foot that stepped on rock.)* Is this the foot?

BELLE: Oh, I thought you were kneeling — Yes, that's the foot.

BEAST: I *am* . . . kneeling . . . Mademoiselle. *(Beast dips cloth into basin of water and washes Belle's feet.)* Water too cold?

BELLE: I have lost my hatred for you, Beast.

BEAST: I am very glad.

BELLE: I hated you because you threatened my father and kept me a prisoner.

BEAST: Would you stay if you weren't a prisoner? . . . Would you stay with someone who . . . looked like . . . me?

BELLE: If I loved him, it wouldn't matter what he looked like.

BEAST: And do you . . . love him?

BELLE: No, Beast. But I am growing fond of you — it's strange. *(Beast dries her feet and puts her slippers on for her.)*

BEAST: Clumsy . . . Sorry.

BELLE: No, you're fine . . . Thank you . . . Sir.

BEAST: I am "sir"? . . . A . . . *man?*

BELLE: Well, you're not a woman, that's for certain.

BEAST: Here. *(Hands her folded up piece of paper.)* I wrote a poem.

BELLE: It's difficult to read — it's so messy. Did you write this by yourself, Beast?

BEAST: *(Holding up paws.)* Yes.

BELLE: Why didn't you use magic?

BEAST: Magic lies.

BELLE: *(Reads.)* As snow melts on a rose
That you are touching,
So my nature softens
And my spirit, blushing
Hides itself in darkness,
Hushing even the smallest
Bird, for fear her
Meager song will chase you
From this garden.

It is very beautiful.

BEAST: Not . . . as . . . beautiful . . . as . . . you, . . . Belle.

BELLE: Beast, are you crying?

BEAST: Yes.

BELLE: What can I do?

BEAST: Marry me, Belle.

BELLE: I can't.

BEAST: I know.

BELLE: Believe me, Beast.

BEAST: I do. *(Exits.)*

The Boy Who Stole the Stars
Julian Wiles

Events unfold when Nicholas visits his grandfather one summer. Grandfather, who is becoming forgetful and isn't as friendly as he used to be, tells Nicholas a story about how if all the stars are taken from the sky and scattered across the earth, paradise will return. When Nicholas learns that his grandfather is dying, he sets on an adventure to capture the stars and slay a dragon.

One Male and One Female

In the first scene, the boy (Nicholas) plays in the yard under the stars, when the freckled-face girl enters; she tells the boy she's sorry his grandfather is ill. In the second scene, the boy speaks of his plan to count the stars and save his grandfather. In the third scene, the freckled-face girl, who is trying to count crickets and frogs, comes to the boy, who is finding it difficult to count all the stars. In the final scene, learning that his grandfather is dying, the boy sets out to steal the stars.

✦ ✦ ✦

Nicholas bounds outside with a baseball bat. He picks up rocks (imaginary) and bats them out toward the audience. After hitting a few times, he notices the first star of the evening.

THE BOY: Twinkle, twinkle, little star
How I wonder what you are
Like a diamond in the sky
Stick a moon beam in your eye.

(He throws a rock at a star.)

THE FRECKLED-FACE GIRL: *(Entering.)* Whatcha doing, Nicholas?

THE BOY: Throwing a rock at a star.

THE FRECKLED-FACE GIRL: That's useful.

THE BOY: What's it to you?

THE FRECKLED-FACE GIRL: Nothing — how's your grandfather?

THE BOY: What do you mean?

THE FRECKLED-FACE GIRL: Nothing — just that my mom said he got lost going to the grocery store and they had to call your grandmother to come pick him up.

THE BOY: He hasn't been feeling well lately.

THE FRECKLED-FACE GIRL: That's what my mom said, only she wasn't so polite.

THE BOY: I'll bet she'd talk differently if it was one of your grandfathers . . .

THE FRECKLED-FACE GIRL: I haven't got any grandfathers, they're both dead — before I was born.

THE BOY: I've only got one left —

THE FRECKLED-FACE GIRL: I'm sorry he's sick.

THE BOY: Me too.

THE FRECKLED-FACE GIRL: Have you decided what you're going to do for your summer science project?

THE BOY: No, not exactly, have you?

THE FRECKLED-FACE GIRL: I've got a couple of great ideas floating around. I'll decide on one by tomorrow.

THE BOY: You're not going to make another papier-mâché volcano are you? There's still soot on the ceiling from that one.

THE FRECKLED-FACE GIRL: That was a good project — I got an A on it.

THE BOY: That's only because you cried after the principal called the fire department. The teacher felt sorry for you.

THE FRECKLED-FACE GIRL: She did not!

THE BOY: If you say so.

THE FRECKLED-FACE GIRL: Well I do, so there . . . *(Starts to exit, turns back.)* Oh, I only came over to tell you that my mom said that we'll pick you up around six forty-five.

THE BOY: Six forty-five! Why so early?

THE FRECKLED-FACE GIRL: When you live out in the country, Nicholas, you have to get used to getting up early, besides, it takes a while to get to school from here.

THE BOY: Six forty-five?

THE FRECKLED-FACE GIRL: Yeah, well, I've got to get home to supper. See you later. *(She exits.)*

THE BOY: *(Calling after her.)* Yeah, later — make it much later. *(He crosses to the stump and pulls out a loop of string and begins making string tricks.)*

✦ ✦ ✦

THE BOY: *(Speaking to his imaginary teacher out front.)*
Yes, ma'am,
my science project?
I plan to count the stars.
Ma'am?
. . . that's right . . . count the stars.
Yes, ma'am, all of them.
. . . well, if it's all right, my grandfather will help me . . .
my grandfather used to be a star counter himself . . .
Ma'am?
A star counter,
you know, on a ship.
He was a navigator.
Yes, ma'am, that's what I said,
a navigator.
What?
Yes, I suppose I will need all the help I can get . . .
Yes, ma'am, I'm sure it's the project I want to do.

(Freckled-face girl enters upstage left and stands just behind and to the side of him.)

. . . well, it's no worse than building papier-mâché volcanos that melt before they erupt . . .

(Freckled-face girl clears her throat, clearly annoyed.)

I'm sorry, but . . .

Yes, ma'am,

next term,

first day of class,

I'll be ready.

THE FRECKLED-FACE GIRL: We'll see.

THE BOY: Don't lose any sleep over it.

THE FRECKLED-FACE GIRL: You don't have to worry about that.

THE BOY: Oh, I forgot, you'll be too busy looking for crickets and frogs, sounds like a great science project.

THE FRECKLED-FACE GIRL: It beats papier-mâché volcanos, don't you think!

THE BOY: Anything beats papier-mâché volcanos.

THE FRECKLED-FACE GIRL: So, you're going to count all the stars.

THE BOY: I thought I would.

THE FRECKLED-FACE GIRL: *(Erasing an imaginary board.)* Why did you decide to count stars?

THE BOY: I thought it would be fun to do something with my grandfather.

THE FRECKLED-FACE GIRL: How is he?

THE BOY: About the same.

THE FRECKLED-FACE GIRL: Was he really a navigator?

THE BOY: He was one of the best. He even went on an expedition to the South Pole.

THE FRECKLED-FACE GIRL: No kidding.

THE BOY: He guided ships around the world twice, and now he can't even get home from the supermarket.

THE FRECKLED-FACE GIRL: I'm sorry about that.

THE BOY: It doesn't matter.

THE FRECKLED-FACE GIRL: Yes it does . . . Look, we all get lost sometimes — when I was a little kid, I remember crying my eyes out once when my mom left me alone in the shopping cart — she was only on the next aisle, but that didn't matter, I cried anyway.

THE BOY: But you were a kid — kids are supposed to get lost and cry — grownups aren't. They're supposed to have it all together, and when they don't people think they're nuts.

THE FRECKLED-FACE GIRL: I suppose you're right.

THE BOY: You know I'm right. Your mother thinks he's nuts.

THE FRECKLED-FACE GIRL: I wouldn't pay too much attention to my mother, I certainly don't.

THE BOY: You know, you can actually be funny sometimes.

THE FRECKLED-FACE GIRL: And you can actually be civilized.

THE BOY: Gee, thanks.

THE FRECKLED-FACE GIRL: Don't mention it. Well, I guess I gotta go.

THE BOY: Right.

THE FRECKLED-FACE GIRL: Bye. *(She exits.)*

THE BOY: Bye . . . Now I've done it . . . she likes me!
(Fade to black.)

✦ ✦ ✦

THE FRECKLED-FACE GIRL: Come on little cricket
come on . . .
. . . there's that other frog I heard.
Come on both of you. I just want to count you.
That's a good boy . . . or girl?
Look out!
Look out little cricket!
Oh, no!
. . . I wonder if I should still count a cricket that's been swallowed by a frog?

Gosh . . .

Think of all those frogs with crickets inside of them.

There's no way to know . . .

unless . . . unless frogs with crickets inside of them jump
farther than . . .

THE BOY: How are the crickets and frogs?

THE FRECKLED-FACE GIRL: All right, I suppose . . . They're . . .
em . . . coming together, so to speak.

THE BOY: That's good, because I'm having a time with these
stars. There are so many it's like starting over every night.

THE FRECKLED-FACE GIRL: At least they don't hop around.

THE BOY: No, but you can catch all the crickets and frogs in the
bog and count them and let them go. I can't do that with
the stars.

THE FRECKLED-FACE GIRL: You could have chosen crickets and
frogs . . . it was your idea to count the stars.

THE BOY: I used to play with frogs when I was little. But I had
enough of them — so slimy and all.

THE FRECKLED-FACE GIRL: As I remember it, you brought that
bullfrog to school and right in front of the whole class he
peed on you . . .

THE BOY: I don't remember that . . .

THE FRECKLED-FACE GIRL: And Jonathan said you'd get warts.

THE BOY: Leave Jonathan out of it.

THE FRECKLED-FACE GIRL: Oh, I forgot, no one can mention
Jonathan around you without your going crazy.

THE BOY: Who said that?

THE FRECKLED-FACE GIRL: Everyone says it.

THE BOY: That's not true.

THE FRECKLED-FACE GIRL: Yes it is . . . they all say you grieve
over him like he was a lost puppy.

THE BOY: They do not . . . you don't know what you're talking
about.

THE FRECKLED-FACE GIRL: And he hasn't written you, has he?

THE BOY: Why should he?

THE FRECKLED-FACE GIRL: I heard you got one Christmas card and that was it — I can't believe you can't forget him.

THE BOY: So he moved away, what does it matter?

THE FRECKLED-FACE GIRL: Doesn't matter at all to me . . . only your friends think you've gone nuts — you don't give any of us the time of day now that Jonathan's gone . . .

THE BOY: Let's drop it, OK?

THE FRECKLED-FACE GIRL: OK . . . how many stars have you counted?

THE BOY: Eight hundred and twenty-seven . . . how many crickets and frogs?

THE FRECKLED-FACE GIRL: Not counting the crickets inside the . . . I mean 213 frogs and 614 crickets, so far. But that's only this side of the bog . . .

THE BOY: Yes, I've got a lot of big constellations to go, too.

THE FRECKLED-FACE GIRL: Will you finish by September?

THE BOY: Certainly, will you?

THE FRECKLED-FACE GIRL: Certainly.

THE BOY: Boy, is she stuck on herself.

THE FRECKLED-FACE GIRL: Boy, is he stuck on himself.
(Fade to black.)

+ + +

Lights up.

THE FRECKLED-FACE GIRL: Wait . . . Where are you going?

THE BOY: What's it to you?

THE FRECKLED-FACE GIRL: Nicholas, what's the matter?

THE BOY: Nothing.

THE FRECKLED-FACE GIRL: What's so terrible about nothing?

THE BOY: Who cares?

THE FRECKLED-FACE GIRL: I do, Nicholas.

THE BOY: My grandfather . . . he's dying, Genevieve.

THE FRECKLED-FACE GIRL: Dying? . . . I don't know what to say.

THE BOY: There's nothing to say — there's nothing to do. It's done, it's decided, it's happening, and there's nothing I can do about it.

THE FRECKLED-FACE GIRL: You love him Nicholas, perhaps that's all he needs.

THE BOY: He doesn't notice that.

THE FRECKLED-FACE GIRL: Must run in the family.

THE BOY: What?

THE FRECKLED-FACE GIRL: In case you haven't noticed, Nicholas, I want to be your friend — have you ever had a friend?

THE BOY: Sure, I had a friend once — a best friend — but he moved away. The next year I got a Christmas card from somebody using his name, but it wasn't the same . . . There, are you satisfied?

THE FRECKLED-FACE GIRL: So you lost a friend. Are you never going to take a chance on another one?

THE BOY: My grandfather's my friend, and now I'm going to lose him, too. It hurts — it hurts too much.

THE FRECKLED-FACE GIRL: Maybe that's the price we have to pay for caring so much.

THE BOY: Then the price is too high.

THE FRECKLED-FACE GIRL: Sometimes we have to reach to the sky to get what we want.

THE BOY: If only we could steal the stars.

THE FRECKLED-FACE GIRL: What?

THE BOY: Anything can become real if you believe it hard enough.

THE FRECKLED-FACE GIRL: Nicholas, you're not making any sense . . . where are you going?

THE BOY: To slay a dragon.

(Blackout.)

The Boy Who Talked to Whales
Webster Smalley

Set near Puget Sound in the Northwest, ten-year-old Jerry befriends and learns to communicate with Ooka, a fifty-foot whale that has escaped from whalers. Together with his friend, Meg, Jerry devises a plan to help Ooka protect herself. In the process, though, they create an international crisis that they have to help the president of the United States resolve.

One Male and Two Females

In the first scene of the play, Betty, Jerry's mother, is searching for him when she encounters eleven-year-old Meg, a friend of Jerry's, playing on the pier. Betty and, at first, Meg are unaware that Jerry is hiding under the pier. In the second scene, Jerry introduces his friend Meg to Ooka, the whale.

Betty sits on edge of pier, hears noise.

BETTY: Jerry!

MEG: *(Entering.)* It's just me.

BETTY: *(Stands.)* Oh, Meg. Have you seen Jerry?
(Meg is eleven, but is in Jerry's class. She is dressed in jeans and a sloppy blouse. She is attractive and bright, a bit of a tomboy.)

MEG: *(Simply.)* I was eating dinner.

BETTY: Well, I want Jerry to have his dinner.

MEG: Yeah, I heard. I wish my dad'd fix interesting things. We just had crummy old steak.

BETTY: Do you know where he might be?

MEG: He might be anywhere.

BETTY: I think you know most of his hiding places.

(Meg has been through this before. She uses evasive tactics, picks up rocks [imaginary], and skips them toward the audience.)

BETTY: *(Understands Meg's motive.)* Meg, what are you doing?

MEG: Skippin' rocks. You gotta hit between the waves or —

BETTY: I see you are skipping rocks.

MEG: *(Innocent.)* Then why ask?

BETTY: Because — *(Realizes she is falling into Meg's trap.)* Meg, you are changing the subject because you don't want to tell me where Jerry might be.

MEG: There are lots and lots of places.

BETTY: That's why I want help. You and Jerry know almost every rock and tree on or near this beach. Last night it was almost eight o'clock — and the night before, it was —

MEG: *(Interrupts.)* He forgets. You know how he is, he gets thinkin' about somethin'.

BETTY: I know, but he needs to eat. Will you find him for me? *(She starts to walk off.)*

MEG: What if I can't?

BETTY: I'm sure you can, if you want to.

MEG: Not if he doesn't want me to, I can't.

BETTY: *(Stops.)* Why wouldn't he want you to find him? You haven't had an argument, have you?

MEG: No, but when he's sort of unhappy, he —

BETTY: *(Concerned.)* Why would be be unhappy? Did something happen?

MEG: He didn't say anything about school?

(Jerry frantically tries to signal Meg, but she fails to see him.)

BETTY: I hardly saw him when he came in, late as usual. He dropped his books and came to the beach. I was on the phone.

(Meg has strolled away and is on her knees sorting through rocks on the beach.)

BETTY: Meg, stop that. You are not really looking for agates. You and Jerry have found every last agate on this part of the beach years ago. You are trying to change the subject.

MEG: The trouble with you, Mrs. Johnson, you always know what I'm doin'. My dad doesn't, and he's s'posed to 'cause he's a psychologist.

BETTY: I was a girl once, Meg. It helps. *(Half to herself.)* The problem is, I was never a boy. Now, tell me. What happened in school?

MEG: You better ask him.

BETTY: Meg Meyer, you are not going to tell me that something happened in school and then not tell me what.

MEG: It would be snitchin'.

BETTY: *(Pauses a moment, realizing Meg's problem, then.)* No. No, it wouldn't. I understand how you feel. But I know something happened, and I'll find out anyway, won't I? So you might as well tell me now.

MEG: *(Reluctantly.)* Well, I didn't talk to him after he was sent to the office.

BETTY: Oh, no! Not to the office again!

(Jerry is signalling Meg to be quiet.)

MEG: *(Not seeing Jerry.)* Yeah. An' after havin' to stand in the hall. It wasn't his best day.

BETTY: *(Resigned.)* What did he do this time?

MEG: Oh, it wasn't bad. He was just practicin' noises. He forgot.

BETTY: Noises? What kind of noises?

MEG: You know. The kind he makes all the time. Code noises.

BETTY: *(Mystified.)* Code noises! What do you mean?

MEG: *(Makes a series of dot-dash sounds, then.)* Like they told us in school. Samuel F. B. Morse invented the telegraph and dots and dashes and —

BETTY: *(Impatient.)* I know Morse invented the telegraph and the code. What did Jerry do?

MEG: He talks in it. Morse code. *(Looking at Betty curiously.)* I thought you knew that.

BETTY: *(Remembering.)* That's what those strange sounds were.

MEG: *(Matter of fact.)* Sure. Morse code. He tried to teach me, but it was too hard.

BETTY: Funny, he didn't tell me. Why would he want to learn the Morse code?

MEG: I asked him that, too. An' did he give a dumb answer. "Because it's there," he said. I think he read that somewhere. He reads a lot — an' not every kid can talk in Morse code. *(She is trying to be helpful.)*

BETTY: *(Trying to put it all together.)* Does Miss Franklin know it was Morse code?

MEG: Naw. Jerry doesn't try to explain things to her. He said it just gets him in more trouble.

BETTY: I've tried to explain Jerry to Miss Franklin, but —

MEG: You can't explain Jerry to Miss Franklin.

BETTY: It's the *kinds* of trouble he gets into. It isn't — the usual kind of trouble.

MEG: Like the mice, huh?

BETTY: I think she almost understood the mice. Lots of children like animals.

MEG: Your car engine?

BETTY: *(A bit defensive.)* That was in the summer. I don't think she knows about that.

MEG: She knows all right. That's why she sends him to sixth-grade science class. How many ten-year-old kids could put a car engine back together?

BETTY: *(Smiles with a certain pride, but —)* Not many, I admit — but it's things like that — and the noises that get him sent to the office.

MEG: *(Not meaning to say this.)* It was the fight that got him sent to the office.

BETTY: Fight!? What fight?

MEG: *(Explaining. Realizing she has let something slip out.)* Noises aren't bad enough to get sent to the office.

BETTY: Meg, did someone start a fight with Jerry?

MEG: *(Pauses. Struggles between loyalty and honesty.)* No.
(Jerry's signals become more frantic.)

BETTY: You just said there was a fight.

MEG: Sure, but — Jerry started it. Fred O'Connell said something about that whale, and Jerry just — Boy, you should have seen him!
(She has finally seen Jerry signalling, and the last words suddenly slow down.)

BETTY: What are you talking about? Whale? Jerry *started* a fight with — *(Realizing with horror.)* Do you mean Fred O'Connell, that great big, huge — !?

MEG: *(Fully aware of Jerry. Very reluctant.)* Well, yes — but you ask Jerry. I gotta go now. *(And she starts off.)*

BETTY: *(Rushing to block Meg's exit.)* Meg Meyer, you are not going to stop there. You tell me everything that happened. If Jerry's in trouble, I can't help if I don't know about it, can I?

MEG: *(Caught between Betty and awareness of Jerry.)* Well — no —

BETTY: *(Firmly.)* Meg?!

MEG: *(Closing her eyes, blurting it out, a tumble of words.)* I didn't hear it all. It was something about Fred's dad going after the whale, and Jerry got all shook. It didn't last long. Fred's lots bigger than Jerry.

BETTY: *(Disbelieving.)* Meg, Jerry doesn't start fights. He doesn't fight.

MEG: He sure did this time. He just closed his eyes and waded right in, both arms goin' like windmills. He's tougher'n you think. Wild! But Fred stopped him pretty quick — then, Miss Franklin came. But it was too late. I dunno why he did it.

BETTY: Calm down, Meg. You said something about a whale? What did a whale have to do with it?

MEG: How do I know? You know how Jerry is about some things? Funny.

BETTY: Some people may think so. Miss Franklin and the principal, but you know and I know he usually has some good reason for what he does. I need you to help me find out what that reason is. Will you?

MEG: I guess — *(Remembers Jerry's presence.)* But what if he doesn't want you to know?

BETTY: *(Starting off.)* You just find him. Tell him I'm making something special for dinner. I'll do the rest.

MEG: *(Reluctantly.)* OK.

+ + +

Betty exits. Meg makes sure she has gone for good, then —

MEG: Jerry, she's gone. *(As he climbs on the pier.)* Why didn't you stay down? She almost saw you. *(No answer. Apologetically.)* I'm sorry about what I said. She kept asking things. I couldn't help it. *(Still no answer.)* You better go in . . . Aren't you going to talk?

JERRY: It was bad enough before. Now she'll ask questions all night.

MEG: She wasn't really mad. Anyway, she knows you weren't hurt.

JERRY: Naw, I know. She just gets curiouser and curiouser. It's even worse since she took those psychology courses at the college. Is your dad like that?

MEG: *(Thoughtful.)* He asks some questions, but he's an adult psychologist. I don't think I have to worry till I grow up . . . Anyway, it's your own fault. Why'd you fight about a stupid old whale?

JERRY: It's not stupid, it's smart. Maybe the smartest, most intelligent whale in the world.

MEG: What're you talkin' about? *(As Jerry gets pipe from under pier.)* Hey, what's that?

JERRY: A pipe. I need to practice.

MEG: Practice? Practice what?

JERRY: I can't talk about what.

MEG: I don't get it.

JERRY: I can't talk about this. It's too important. *(Accusing.)* You told her about the Morse code.

MEG: I thought you'd told her yourself. I had to say something about the noises you make. You know something? They don't even sound like the Morse code anymore.

JERRY: I know.

MEG: You mean they're not the Morse code? What are they then?

JERRY: Can't tell. It's a secret.

MEG: *(Indicating pipe.)* Like that?

JERRY: That's right. I can't tell even you.

MEG: I won't tell anyone — not anyone — not ever. Who else can you tell besides me? . . . Not anyone, that's who . . . Please?

JERRY: *(Realizes the truth of this.)* It's so hard to keep it all inside me. *(Deadly earnest.)* You really promise? Not a little promise, probably the biggest promise you ever made, ever in your life.

MEG: I promise — biggest ever in my whole life.

JERRY: *(A pause, then decides.)* All right. I'll show you.

MEG: *(Lost.)* Show me? Show me what?

JERRY: The secret. Watch! And listen.

(At the end of the pier, he places one end of the pipe in the water and puts his mouth to the other.)

MEG: What are you doing?

JERRY: Wait! You'll see.

(Puts his mouth back to pipe, and with much effort and breath, he begins to make strange and wonderful deep musical noises. Meg watches, puzzled.)

MEG: Good grief! What are you doing?

JERRY: *(Breathless.)* Sh-hh. Wait.

(He makes more noises, then listens to the pipe.)

MEG: *(Can't stand the wait.)* You have to tell me. I can't guess.

JERRY: *(Still listening.)* Sh-h-h.

(He gestures for quiet, then a distant splash is heard on the house speaker. Jerry makes more noises. Other splashes as he holds his hand up for silence. Then, a short whale song from Ooka.)

MEG: *(Whispers in wonderment.)* Holy cow, what is it?

JERRY: *(Simply, just explaining a fact.)* A whale. The biggest whale you ever saw. Her name is Ooka.

MEG: *(Astounded, but not doubting Jerry.)* A real whale? A genuine, big whale — that sings? *(Gen-u-wine.)*

JERRY: Of course. They all talk like that. An' she isn't a killer whale, or even a gray whale like they think. She's a sperm whale.

(Ooka's answering song is heard.)

I have to warn her — about Mr. O'Connell's boats. That's what's so important. *(He makes sounds into pipe.)* There! *(Whale sounds diminish in distance as he gets his breath.)* Now, she won't be there if Mr. O'Connell goes after her. *(And he moves to hide the pipe.)*

MEG: She — won't be there?

JERRY: *(Simply, as he hides pipe.)* I told her to go away from here for a while.

MEG: *(Following him as he moves away from pier.)* You — *told* — her?

JERRY: That's what I was saying into the pipe. *(Simple expla-*

nation.) Oh, she can't hear me without the pipe. You see, it goes under water and —

MEG: *(Interrupting. One thing at a time.)* You talked — to a — whale!?!!!

JERRY: *(Worried.)* You promised — really promised — not to tell. I'm in enough trouble. On top of everything, I ripped my jeans when Fred O'Connell knocked me down — and Mom hasn't found them yet. More questions!

MEG: You really talked to a whale?!

JERRY: Yeah, I did, but it's only going to get me in more trouble, especially after Mr. O'Connell finds — *(Stops suddenly. He shouldn't have said that.)*

MEG: *(Suspicious.)* Mr. O'Connell finds out what?

JERRY: Nothin' you need to know. Remember, you promised not to tell!

MEG: Ye-es, but — *(No nonsense. Look him in the eye.)* How do you know it's a whale? A sperm whale?

JERRY: She told me — or tried to. Then, I got some whale books from the library — after she jumped. She jumped once — real early in the morning so I could see her. No one was around.

MEG: *(Doubtful, now that it has come to details.)* How do you understand — and talk to a whale? Tell me that.

JERRY: *(At a loss. He doesn't fully understand, himself.)* I don't know. I just — *can.* . . . You see, I sneaked out here one Saturday morning, about a month ago — it was too early for Mom to let me go swimming, and —

MEG: *(Scolding.)* You went swimming alone. That was dumb.

JERRY: *(Quickly.)* I didn't go out deep. Nobody else was up — not even you. So be still and let me talk. *(Acting it out as he remembers. Lies on back.)* I was floating on my back — with my ears under water — and I heard this sound — boo-oo, boo-oo. It was *in* the water. Then, I heard it again, boo-oo.

I was scared. The *water* was making a noise. I stood up quick — and listened. You know what?

MEG: For gosh sakes, tell me.

JERRY: I didn't hear anything.

MEG: *(Annoyed.)* That's not all, and you know it.

JERRY: I ducked my head, and there it was again. All around. *in* the water. *(Another dramatic pause.)*

MEG: You make me mad. Either tell me or I'm going home.

JERRY: OK, OK. I couldn't stay with my head under all day, could I? Besides, I was getting cold. So I put on my clothes and tried to figure it out. That's why the pipe.

MEG: You don't make any sense, Jerry Johnson. Sometimes I think you're as nutty as lots of people think you are. What does a pipe have to do with noises in the water?

JERRY: *(Gets the pipe.)* Don't you see? I remembered this old plastic pipe in the garage. It's like a glass you put on the floor or wall — and you can hear on the other side. Like those things doctors use to listen.

MEG: Stethoscope!

JERRY: Yeah. So, when I put one end in the water, I heard the sounds again. With the pipe.

MEG: *(Takes pipe and listens in water.)* I don't hear anything.

JERRY: She's gone away. Remember? Anyhow, with the pipe, it wasn't so scary. I could listen — slow — and there was a kind of pattern — like in Morse code. I'd come down at night — and real early, even before the sun. I began to understand a little — and I tried to talk with it — and I practiced the sounds. I practiced a lot — even at school.

MEG: I know. You made Miss Franklin want to fly out the window, an' she sort of likes you.

JERRY: You think I'd tell her? Or the principal? *(Imitating principal.)* "Why were you making strange noises, young man?" — Well, sir, I was practicing talking whale. — "Bonkers, young man. You are bonkers. Sorry, we will have to send you away to the Bonkers Farm."

MEG: *(Giggling.)* I can just see Mr. Moffett.

JERRY: Grownups wouldn't understand. Maybe even kids'd think I was crazy. But it's true, I can — *(Grabs her arm, excited.)* I can understand, and talk it a little. You should hear her. Wow! Sometimes she just sings. Ooka likes to sing, just for the fun of it. She has a good voice, don't you think? For a whale?

MEG: *(Thinks a moment.)* I guess. I haven't heard any other whales.

JERRY: She's pretty young.

MEG: *(Suspicious again.)* How do you know it's a girl?

JERRY: It's partly a guess. She wants to have baby whales — like her mother. Her mother got hurt — killed maybe — by a whaler. It's hard to understand what she means. First, I have to try to understand *what* she is saying . . . Then, I have to pretend *I'm* a whale to figure out what she means. *(He begins imitating a whale, using his arms as flukes, and looks up as if from beneath a boat.)* A boat looks a lot different to a whale than to us.

MEG: *(Imitating Jerry, looking up as if at boat.)* Yeah — gee, I hadn't thought of that.

JERRY: *(Excited. Acting it out.)* She loves the big ocean. Go down deep, way down into the dark — then up fast — like flying — and swish — way up in the sunlight. Then *splash* — a big breath and down again and find a nice big, tender octopus to munch — whish — up into the sun and good, fresh air to breathe.

MEG: Octopus — ugh!

JERRY: When she jumped for me, you should have seen her. She is big — I mean, BIG! *(Eyes alight.)* She's bigger than a — a house trailer. When she jumped, she just kept coming out of the water, and coming out — almost forever. *(Earnestly.*

Tears almost come.) She is the most wonderful thing I have ever seen. I love her!

MEG: *(Impressed, but not knowing quite how to respond.)* Jerry, you — You're something!

JERRY: *(Darkly.)* But she's scared.

MEG: What could a big thing like that be scared of?

JERRY: Whalers. That's why she's in Puget Sound, to get away from whaling ships. Then, old Mr. O'Connell — *(A reminder of a big worry.)* Oh — no —

MEG: What? *(As Jerry sits despondently.)* What's the matter? You said something before about Mr. O'Connell.

JERRY: When he finds out, I'm in real trouble.

MEG: When Mr. O'Connell finds out what?

JERRY: When Fred said his dad was going to take his boats and go after Ooka — to try to catch her — something terrible might happen to her. Oh, they couldn't catch her — not her. They don't know how big she is. They think she's an old gray whale. But they'd scare her, even hurt her maybe. Boats are always hurting whales.

MEG: OK. So what'd you do to Mr. O'Connell?

JERRY: I — I sort of took something.

MEG: *(Puzzled.)* You took something? What? Who from?

JERRY: From Mr. O'Connell's boats. Something from their motors. They won't go, now.

MEG: *(Shocked.)* You stole something from Mr. O'Connell's boats? From all three of them?

JERRY: Don't say it like that. I sort of — borrowed some — fuel pumps. *(Hastily.)* I'll give them back as soon as —

MEG: You sto — I mean took the fuel pumps from all three of his boats?

JERRY: *(Nods.)* I don't think he can get replacements right away. But Ooka's in trouble. I had to do it.

MEG: But you told Ooka to go away. She's gone! You didn't have to do that.

JERRY: I wasn't sure I could get her to go. She doesn't always understand. I had to do everything I could, didn't I? Besides, I don't know how far she's gone. See?

MEG: I guess. *(A horrible thought.)* Jerry, he'll know who did it. After you told Fred you'd stop his father.

JERRY: *(Sadly, resigned.)* I know. Fred saw me leaving the boats, too. I told you it was worse than my torn jeans.

Dogbrain
Michael Weller

Nicholas, an inventive six-year-old, gets into trouble when he conjures up an imaginary creature (Dogbrain) to take the blame for his own bad behavior. Visible only to Nicholas, at first Nick is entertained by Dogbrain's antics, but soon the creature creates havoc for Nicholas's family and forces Nicholas and his brother, Tommy, out of the house to fend for themselves in the streets. Once on the streets, the brothers encounter a bag person and a huge dog. But just when events seem out of control, help springs from Nicholas's imagination in the form of Goodybags, a rescuer, who traps Dogbrain and drives him back into Nicholas. Nicholas discovers that he is capable of both good and bad and that he must control his urges.

Two Males

In the following scene, Nick and his brother, Tommy, ride along on bicycles as Dogbrain hip-hops alongside of them, shadowboxing, singing tunelessly. Suddenly a large German shepherd leaps out at them.

+ + +

Street at night. Nick and Tom ride bicycles, scared. Dogbrain hippity-hops along in front of them, shadow boxing, singing tunelessly.

DOGBRAIN: HOORAY
        HOORAY! *(Sung like an echo.)*
        WE'RE RUNNING AWAY

NICK AND DOGBRAIN: WE'RE RUNNING AWAY
   TODAY
   TODAY! *(Sung like an echo.)*
TOM: Where are we going?
NICK: Just . . . away, OK? Far away.
DOGBRAIN: I WONDER WHAT
   THEY'LL SAY,
   THEY'LL SAY?! *(Sung like an echo.)*
   MOM AND DAD,
   TODAY
   TODAY! *(Sung like an echo.)*
   WHEN THEY DISCOVER
   WE'VE RUN AWAY.
   I'LL BET THEY CRY ALL NIGHT AND DAY.
   HOORAY, HOORAY, HOORAY!!!
TOM: What if we get lost, and no one can ever find us again?
DOGBRAIN: What a dumb-dumb!
NICK: I'll take care of you, Tommy.
TOM: What if we get 'tacked by mobsters and dragons?
DOGBRAIN: You think I'm afraid of stuff like that?
NICK: No problem, Tommy . . . I'll protect you. *(To Dogbrain, hand on head.)* You're sure about that?
DOGBRAIN: I'll bite their heads off . . .
NICK: *(To Tom.)* I'll bite their heads off.
DOGBRAIN: I'll kick them in the behind.
NICK: I'll kick them in the behind!
DOGBRAIN: I'll punch them in the privates and rip them and bang them with a hammer until they turn into mush.
NICK: I'm not afraid of anything.
TOM: When I'm six and two halves and a half, I'm gonna be brave like you.
   (Nick starts to turn corner. Tom stops.)
   Come on, this way!
TOM: Isn't this the street where Mister Dimple lives?

NICK: So what?

DOGBRAIN: Let's leave Stupid Tom behind.

TOM: Doesn't he have a great big German leopard?

NICK: A great big what?

TOM: I'm afraid of them.

DOGBRAIN: He's afraid of everything. Let's get going.

NICK: *(Trying to understand.)* What's a German leopard?

TOM: With big teeth, and it barks.

DOGBRAIN: *(Suddenly apprehensive.)* What?

NICK: A German shepherd?

> *(Huge German shepherd leaps out of darkness. Nick and Tom scream and leap on bikes, pedaling furiously while dog lopes in pursuit, growling and barking. Dogbrain exits.)*

TOM: Look out!!!

NICK: Dogbrain, get him, bang his head, twist his tail!

TOM: Faster, Nick . . .

NICK: Go, go . . . he's falling behind, we're losing him!

> *(They finally outpedal dog and stop.)*

TOM: Is he gone?

> *(They listen. Dogbrain enters, boxing the air.)*

DOGBRAIN: I showed that pitiful pooch a thing or two!

NICK: You ran away.

DOGBRAIN: Me? Never! I pinched his nose, I pulled his tail, I stuck him in the ribs; I'm SuperDogbrain!!!

NICK: You're full of hot air is what you are. You're a coward!!!! . . .

DOGBRAIN: I can beat up a grizzly bear if I feel like it. I can pull airplanes out of the sky . . .

NICK: Useless, dumb old Dogbrain . . .

DOGBRAIN: Woof-woof-woof.

> *(Nick circles stage looking for German shepherd.)*

TOM: I'm hungry.

NICK: Here's an apple.

DOGBRAIN: I'm hungry, too. *(Spots.)* Garbage!!! Cat poop, yummy.

NICK: Gross.

(Nick and Tom sit to eat.)

TOM: Can you really *see* Dogbrain? For really real?

DOGBRAIN: Wet, muddy newspaper, super delectable!

NICK: I wish I couldn't. I wish he'd go away. He's gross, and dumb plus he's a coward.

DOGBRAIN: I'm only what *you* are.

NICK: But I'm other things, too. And you're not.

TOM: Will you let me see him one day?

NICK: I can't.

TOM: Why not?

NICK: That's the rules, OK? I just can't.

TOM: Just tell me why, OK?

DOGBRAIN: I want that Stupid Tom to stop flapping his gums, and let me eat my garbage in peace!

(Dogbrain bangs him repeatedly on head. Tom yells with pain as Nick calls out.)

NICK: Stop it. I said stop it. He's afraid, don't hit him . . .

(Tom runs, hides.)

Why didn't you stop when I said stop?

DOGBRAIN: You always let me when I was *inside* you!

NICK: I couldn't see what it looked like.

DOGBRAIN: *(Taunting.)* "I couldn't see what it looked like!"

NICK: The rule is supposed to be you have to do what I want you to. If I say stop, you have to stop.

DOGBRAIN: You *said* stop, but you thought "hit him"! Thought is a "want-to." The rule is I do what you *want to do.*

NICK: I don't like these rules.

DOGBRAIN: Tough bananas.

NICK: *(Looks around.)* Tom? *(Calls.)*

Tom!!!

DOGBRAIN: *(Spots.)* Ooooo, a slimy rat . . . yum-yummy-yum!!!

(Dogbrain stalks rat. Tom peeks out.)

TOM: Is *he* still here?

(Dogbrain pounces and stuffs rat into mouth, chomping with exaggeration.)

NICK: *(Disgusted.)* He's *still* here.

DOGBRAIN: *(Pointing to his mouth.)* I wish he'd stop moving around in my mouth, dumb old rat.

TOM: Take me home.

NICK: Please, stay with me.

TOM: I don't like being owied.

NICK: I don't want to be alone. I'm sorry I ever hit you. I'm sorry I ever hit anyone. I'm sorry I ever thought up Dogbrain.

DOGBRAIN: That was the most succulent rodent I ever ate. If I could add some dead goldfish on a piece of moldy rotten bread and put the rat *between* — mm, a dead-rat and stinky-goldfish sandwich!!!

NICK: Please, go away, Dogbrain.

TOM: Please, take me home, Nick.

NICK: In the morning, OK? Just spend one night. We'll put our bikes behind the wall and pull some garbage cans around us so no one knows we're here, and then we'll be safe.

DOGBRAIN: Garbage?! Did someone say garbage?

TOM: My bloot's gone. I want to go home . . .

DOGBRAIN: "Balloon, Stupid Tom."

(Tom cries.)

NICK: I'll get you another bloot tomorrow. And I'll tell you a bedtime story, just like Dad.

TOM: OK . . .

(They walk bikes behind wall.)

DOGBRAIN: Hey, what's going on?

NICK: Lie down right there.

TOM: What if someone finds us, like a baggage person?

DOGBRAIN: Bag! Bag! It's "bag person!!!"

NICK: This time *I'll* protect you.

TOM: Promise?

NICK: Yeah. Lie down, OK?

DOGBRAIN: Would somebody mind telling me what this is all about?

(Nick and Tom lie down.)

NICK: This is a story about when Nick and Tom ran away from home . . .

DOGBRAIN: Let's do something bad.

TOM: Where did they go?

NICK: Oh, Dogville, Oyster Bay, Bear Mountain . . .

TOM: I'm a-scared of bears.

DOGBRAIN: Let's let the air out of every tire on the street.

NICK: They went to heaven, too. And guess what they found there?

TOM: I give up.

NICK: Tom's balloon.

TOM: *(Pleased.)* For real?

DOGBRAIN: Excuse me, over here, guys.

NICK: Where do you think balloons go when you let go of them? They float up to heaven, of course. They sky there is all balloons, every color, and the strings hang down so you can just reach up and grab the one you want.

TOM: Cool!

DOGBRAIN: I'm *talking* to you, Nicholas.

NICK: And I'm *ignoring* you, Dogbrain.

DOGBRAIN: Oh, yeah?! You can't do that.

NICK: Just watch me . . .

TOM: I like this story. It's almost as good as Daddy tells.

DOGBRAIN: If you try to shut me out, I'll do something loud and bangie to make you look, something like . . .

(Dogbrain loudly bangs garbage-can lid.)

Doors
Suzan L. Zeder

Doors examines the impact of divorce and separation in the lives of young people. Seen through the eyes of eleven-year-old Jeff, the day his parents decide to get a divorce painfully unfolds. Rather than face the reality of the impending divorce, however, Jeff escapes into a fantasy world where he lives in an ideal, happy family. Once his parents honestly confront their own issues, they are able to help him realize that he is not the cause of the divorce, and together they work out a compromise for moving forward.

Two Males

In the first scene, Jeff has just lost his temper and smashed a toy model because of his parents' incessant fighting. His friend Sandy arrives and attempts to turn his interest back to a script they've been writing. In the second scene, Sandy gets Jeff to act out his parents' arguments.

Sandy is heard pounding on the small door.

SANDY: *(Off.)* Jeff, you in there! Jeff? *(Sandy enters through the small door. He is a bit put out, and he lugs a life-sized dummy with him.)*

SANDY: Jeeze, Jeff, doesn't anyone around here answer the door? I've been out there about a half an hour ringing the bell and yelling. Hey, do you know the TV is on? *(Jeff pulls himself together but avoids looking at Sandy.)*

JEFF: Yeah.

SANDY: And the stereo, too? *(Sandy turns off the TV.)* This much noise will rot your brain, at least that's what my mom says. *(Sandy starts to turn off stereo.)*

JEFF: Don't.

SANDY: Can't I at least turn it down? *(Jeff looks toward the large door. Sandy turns it down but not off.)*

JEFF: What are you doing in here?

SANDY: I knew you were home and the front door was unlocked so I . . .

JEFF: What do you want?

SANDY: We've got to finish the script, remember?

JEFF: Look, Sandy, this isn't a good time.

SANDY: Don't you even want to see what I brought?

JEFF: What's that? *(Sandy holds up the dummy proudly.)*

SANDY: It's a body for the crash scene! I figure we could put ketchup all over it for blood and maybe some dog food for brains.

JEFF: That's gross.

SANDY: Wait until you hear how I got it.

JEFF: Sandy . . . *(Sandy acts this out as he goes along.)*

SANDY: I was downtown in this alley behind Nordstroms, and I saw this arm sticking out of a dumpster . . . OH MY! I thought some bum had crawled in there and died, but then I figured out that it was a dummy. So, I asked this big goon by the loading dock if I could have it. And he said, "It'll cost you a dollar." So I grabbed it and ran down Fifth like I was kidnapping it or something. Then this number fourteen bus came along, and I hopped on. The driver said, "You can't bring that thing on this bus!" So, I said, "How dare you insult my younger brother!" And I paid two fares, sat it next to me, and talked to it all the way over here. Man, everyone on that bus really thought I was weird.

JEFF: You are weird. *(Jeff turns away.)*

SANDY: You're the weird one. I thought that would really crack you up. All the way over here, I just kept thinking, this will really crack Jeff up! *(No response.)* What's the matter?

JEFF: Nothing.

SANDY: Your report card! Your parents hit the ceiling about that F in science.

JEFF: I never showed it to them.

SANDY: The dog! You finally asked them if you could have a dog, and they said no, and . . .

JEFF: I haven't asked them about that yet.

SANDY: Then what's wrong? *(Sounds can be heard from behind the door.)*

JEFF: Sandy, I'll come over to your house later and . . .

SANDY: Did you get the video camera from your dad?

JEFF: Uhhhh, he's been out of town.

SANDY: You mean you haven't even asked him yet?

JEFF: I'll ask him.

SANDY: We've got to start shooting tomorrow!

JEFF: I'll ask him later.

SANDY: All right! How's the star ship coming along?

JEFF: *(Pointing towards the door.)* It's over there.

(Sandy crosses to the door and picks up the wrecked model.)

SANDY: What happened to the star ship?

JEFF: It got hit by a meteor shower!

SANDY: It got hit by something! Jeff, the wings are all broken and the frame is cracked! These things cost a lot of money!

JEFF: I'll pay you back! I'll buy you another one! What more do you want?

SANDY: Jeff, we are supposed to be doing this together, and all you're doing is screwing up! *(More sounds are heard.)*

JEFF: I don't want to do this today! Go home, Sandy. I'll call you later.

SANDY: I'm not leaving until we finish the script! And I'm turning that thing off! *(Sandy switches off the stereo; for a second the sounds of the argument can be heard, Sandy hears it and chooses to ignore it. Jeff turns away. Sandy pulls some pages out of his pocket.)*

SANDY: OK, we start with a long shot of the ship hurtling toward the death asteroid. Then we show the crash . . . This will work great! *(He sarcastically holds the model up.)* Then we show the crew, those who haven't been burned alive or had their heads split open . . . *(He indicates the dummy.)* . . . struggling out of the wreck. *(Sandy acts this out as he goes along; Jeff watches, becoming more and more involved.)*

SANDY: Colonel McCabe is the first one out; that's me. Then comes Rocco, the navigator; that's Paul; and then the ship's doctor, old blood and guts; that's Rick; and finally comes the ship's robot computer, CB 430; that's you. . . . *(Jeff suddenly joins in.)*

JEFF: Suddenly, the robot computer starts acting strangely. His lights flash and smoke comes out of his ears. He walks toward the ship's doctor and grabs him . . . *(Jeff grabs the dummy.)* He punches him in the stomach, hits him in the head, crushes him in his steel grip, and throws his lifeless body to the ground. *(Jeff beats the dummy and throws it.)*

SANDY: *(Laughing.)* Rick's not going to like that.

JEFF: Then he whirls around and walks toward Rocco. *(Jeff turns in a circle and grabs the dummy again.)* He grabs him by the arms and twists them out of their sockets! He throws him on the ground, time after time, after time, after time. *(Jeff beats the dummy on the floor.)*

SANDY: Jeff?

JEFF: *(Totally carried away.)* He kicks him in the stomach, in the back, in the head, in the nuts!

SANDY: Jeff, that's not in the script.

JEFF: Finally, he turns on Captain McCabe. *(Jeff turns on him and stalks him.)*

SANDY: Cut it out, Jeff.

JEFF: Coming at him, slowly, slowly . . .

SANDY: I said, cut it out.

JEFF: Closer and closer. *(Jeff moves in and Sandy grows alarmed.)*

SANDY: Stop it!

JEFF: He raises his arm . . .

SANDY: Jeff! *(Jeff backs him up until he is next to the bed.)*

JEFF: And zap! The death ray! Colonel McCabe collapses in agony.

(Sandy is forced down on the bed. He is angry and confused.)

SANDY: He does not.

JEFF: He does too.

SANDY: Colonel McCabe does not die! It says in the script, I don't die!

JEFF: You will if I want you to.

SANDY: I will not!

JEFF: Who's got the camera?

SANDY: I don't know, Jeff. Who does? *(Jeff turns away.)* You're such a jerk! I'm going home!

JEFF: Get out of here!

SANDY: I am!

JEFF: And take this piece of junk with you! *(Jeff throws the dummy at Sandy.)* Go home to your mommy and daddy, clear out of here and leave me alone!

SANDY: You're a stupid jerk, Jeff. You've been acting like a stupid jerk ever since your parents first started . . .

JEFF: You shut up about my parents! You don't know anything about my parents!

SANDY: I know that they're yelling again, Jeff, I've heard them ever since I've been here. I could even hear them down on the street.

JEFF: Get out of here, Sandy!

SANDY: I know all about it. *(Jeff turns away.)* My mom told me. Your mom talks to my mom; they gab all the time.

JEFF: *(Without turning to him.)* What did she say?

SANDY: She said that there was trouble over here, and I should keep my big nose out of it. *(Jeff sits, upset. Sandy hesitates and approaches cautiously.)* You want to talk about it in the pact?

JEFF: The pact?

SANDY: You remember the pact, Jeff?

JEFF: We were just little kids.

SANDY: You remember how we both pissed on that dead frog and buried it? How we both cut our fingers and spit and swore with our blood that we would always tell each other everything?

JEFF: We were just little kids.

SANDY: Yeah.

JEFF: *(After a pause.)* I don't care anymore, Sandy. They can scream at each other until they're hoarse, I don't care. They can slap each other around all day, I don't care. I just want it to stop.

SANDY: Do they really hit each other?

JEFF: I don't know. I don't care!

SANDY: Jeeze, I don't know what I'd do if my parents ever hit each other.

JEFF: I didn't say they did. I just said, I didn't care.

SANDY: Do you ever see them?

JEFF: I never see anything, it's always behind the door.

SANDY: Do they ever come down for breakfast in the morning, you know, with black eyes or bruises?

JEFF: Blow it out your ear, Sandy.

SANDY: Do you know what it's about?

JEFF: Nobody tells me anything.

SANDY: Do you know when it started?

JEFF: I knew something was up when they started having all

these appointments. When I'd ask Mom where she was going, she'd say, "Your father and I have an appointment."

✦ ✦ ✦

Jeff beats his hand on the table.

JEFF: I hate breakfast.

SANDY: Maybe you shouldn't have read at the table.

JEFF: It wouldn't have made any difference.

SANDY: My parents do that kind of thing all the time. It's like they have a secret code or something, they don't even have to talk, they read each other's minds.

JEFF: It used to be that way with my folks too; but now it's like they are screaming at each other, but their voices are so high pitched that only dogs can hear them.

SANDY: Jeeze. *(There is a pause and voices can be heard from behind the door. Jeff turns away. Sandy is a bit curious.)*

SANDY: Jeff, do you ever, you know, listen?

JEFF: Huh?

SANDY: I mean, when they fight, do you, you know, try to hear what they're saying?

JEFF: Sandy, I spend most of my time trying not to hear.

SANDY: Well, sometimes my folks argue, they don't really fight or anything; but when they argue, part of me tries to shut it out and part of me really wants to know what's going on.

JEFF: *(Not unkindly.)* You little creep!

SANDY: No, but the weird thing is, the really weird thing is, whenever I listen, it all sounds so stupid! Like last year, you know, we all went down to Puyallup, to the fair. We go every year, and every year the same thing happens. *(Sandy uses a couple of chairs to set up a "car" and he plays out the following.)* My dad always drives and my mom sits next to him and does needlepoint. Julie, Carrie, and I sit in the back seat and argue over who has to sit on the hump. After we have been driving for about a half an hour, my mom looks up and says, "We always go this way and we always get lost."

Then my dad says, "You have a better route?"

And my mom says, "Back there at the service station, I told you to turn left."

"But that's the way all the traffic goes."

"That's because it's the right way."

"There's less traffic this way."

"THAT'S because we're going to Auburn."

Then, Julie says, "But I thought we were going to the fair!"

And they both say, "Be quiet, Julie."

And my mom says, "Daddy's trying to drive."

And Dad says, "What's that supposed to mean?"

So, my mom says, "It's not supposed to mean anything. I am just trying to get us to the fair. If you'd listen instead of charging ahead, we wouldn't be lost."

Then Dad says, "Who's lost? I know exactly where we are."

And Mom says, "OK, where are we?"

And we all say, "WE'RE LOST!" Then they both turn around and yell at US.

JEFF: Did you get to the fair?

SANDY: Yeah.

JEFF: How was it?

SANDY: It was great.

JEFF: With my folks we'd never get there. *(Jeff takes Sandy's place and acts out the following.)*

JEFF: My mom would say, "The reason you're driving this way is because you really don't want to go to the fair."

And my dad would say, "What?"

"You didn't want to go last night when I suggested it and you didn't want to go this morning, when I was packing the picnic. That's why you didn't help."

"You said, you didn't need any help."

"Still, it would have been nice."

"Nice? I'm being nice. I'm taking you to the fair, aren't I?"

"Only because you feel guilty."

"Guilty?"

"Because you didn't take us last year."

"But I'm taking you this year! I am taking you to the god-damned fair when I should be at the office."

"See, I knew you didn't want to go."

Then, we'd turn around and all the way back to Seattle all you'd hear would be the sound of ice melting in the cooler.

SANDY: Did that really happen?

JEFF: No, but that's what would have happened.

SANDY: How do you know?

JEFF: I know, believe me, I know.

SANDY: What do you know?

JEFF: I know that's what would have happened.

SANDY: That's not what I mean. What do you know about what's happening?

JEFF: I don't know.

SANDY: You don't know what you know?

JEFF: No! What are you talking about?

SANDY: Look Jeff, if you can figure out what's going on, then maybe you can do something about it.

JEFF: I've tried.

SANDY: Well, try again! What are the facts?

JEFF: You sound like something out of "Magnum, P.I."*

*(*Update to any popular police or detective show and have Sandy imitate the lead character in his inquisition.)*

SANDY: I'm just trying to help. *(Sandy leaps to his feet and becomes a detective.)* Come on, man, what do you know?

JEFF: I know my dad's not sleeping at home at night.

SANDY: OK, where does he go?

JEFF: I don't know.

SANDY: Well, if he's not sleeping at home, he has to be sleeping somewhere else.

JEFF: Brilliant.

SANDY: Have you asked him?

JEFF: No.

SANDY: Why not?

JEFF: I can really see me going up to my father and saying, "Where you been sleeping these days, Dad?" Get real.

SANDY: We may have to tail him.

JEFF: I'm not going to do that!

SANDY: It was just a suggestion. Say, Jeff, do you think he's got a . . . girlfriend.

JEFF: No.

SANDY: Why not?

JEFF: He just wouldn't!

SANDY: OK, scratch that. What else do you know?

JEFF: I know they fight a lot.

SANDY: What about?

JEFF: Everything . . . anything.

SANDY: You must have heard something in particular.

JEFF: This afternoon, I heard my mom say, "I'm not giving up."

SANDY: Giving up what?

JEFF: I couldn't hear.

SANDY: Smoking! Your dad wants her to give up smoking!

JEFF: She doesn't smoke.

SANDY: When my mom tried to give up smoking, she threw a whole plate of spaghetti at my dad. She said it slipped, but I knew she threw it.

JEFF: I said, she doesn't smoke.

SANDY: You sure?

JEFF: She's my mother!

SANDY: What else did you hear?

JEFF: I heard my mom say something about a job.

SANDY: YOUR DAD LOST HIS JOB!

JEFF: I don't think . . .

SANDY: That's it! Jeff, I saw this thing on "Sixty Minutes," about how all these people are losing jobs. First they lose the job, then they go on welfare, then everybody starts fighting with everybody and . . .

JEFF: My dad works for himself, he's a contractor.

SANDY: Oh no, Jeff! That's the worst.

JEFF: But he just started a new project over in Bellevue . . .

SANDY: Don't take my word, ask Mike Wallace!

JEFF: Do you really think . . .

SANDY: Here, I'll show you. *(Sandy grabs the dummy and mimes the characters with it.)* Here is your father, sitting around reading his paper. And your mother comes in and says, "Well, I certainly hope that you're looking for a job." And he says, "Job, I have a job." And she says, "I mean a job with some money!" "Maybe if you wouldn't spend so much on cigarettes and panty hose . . ."

JEFF: I told you, she doesn't . . .

SANDY: And she says, "Me spend so much? You're such a cheapskate . . ."

JEFF: Sandy . . .

SANDY: And that really makes him mad so he hauls off and . . . Bam! SLAP! POW! THWACK! *(Sandy makes the dummy punch the air. Jeff grabs it from him.)*

JEFF: I never said they hit each other!

SANDY: I was just trying to . . .

JEFF: I've never seen them hit each other. They're not like that at all! *(There is a pause.)*

SANDY: Hey, Jeff, why don't you just ask them what's going on? *(Jeff tenderly carries the dummy over to the bed.)* Ask your mom, she'll tell you something. My mother always tells me something.

JEFF: I just want it to stop, Sandy. That's all I really want. Every night when I hear them in there, I put the pillow over my head, so I can't hear them and I try to imagine what it would be like if they would just stop fighting. I try to make myself dream about it. If they would just stop fighting, everything would be perfect. *(Jeff covers the dummy's head with a pillow during this speech. Lights change and there is music as we move into his fantasy.)* It would be morning, and the first thing I hear would be Mom, in the kitchen making breakfast. The first thing I would smell would be bacon frying. The first thing I feel would be sunlight on my face.

Early Man
Hannah Vincent

Set in contemporary England, *Early Man* tells the story of Sam, a teenage girl for whom life is proving to have more than its share of knocks — that is until she meets a new friend in a most unusual way. While visiting a museum on a field trip, she discovers that she is able to communicate with Bog Boy, whose remains are in a glass case. Bog Boy tells Sam about his life and seeks her help in bringing him a brooch that his girlfriend, Hagaar, had given him. Sam sets out to fulfill Bog Boy's dream, whatever it takes.

One Male and One Female

Here, Sam, who is visiting the museum, aproaches Bog Boy to find out if he is real. Later, Bog Boy tells Sam of his girlfriend, Hagaar.

✦ ✦ ✦

Sam approaches Bog Boy.

SAM: Are you real?
BOG BOY: Course I'm real.
SAM: How did you get here?
BOG BOY: They brought me, didn't they.
SAM: Who?
BOG BOY: The Museum People. Dig dig dig. Load of rustling and shuffling. Stamping. Voices, then quiet. Gently — ever so gentle, but even the tiniest movement felt like thunder. My

arms . . . my legs . . . carried me like a baby and brought me here.

SAM: I don't understand . . . where were you?

BOG BOY: Not far from here. It's a place . . . we used to call it Willow Walk.

SAM: I know Willow Walk! I live just round the corner!

BOG BOY: It was our special place. That's what we called it. There was a willow tree . . .

SAM: Not any more there ain't. It's all houses.

(Silence.)

What was it like before they dug you up?

BOG BOY: Like being asleep. Nice. Nice and warm.

SAM: Miss Stringer tells us off if we say nice. Says it's not a proper word.

BOG BOY: Course it's a proper word — what's not proper about it?

(Sam shrugs.)

SAM: My dog died. When I buried him I put his blanket in it to keep him warm.

BOG BOY: Was he yours?

(Sam nods.)

SAM: Got him when I was little.

BOG BOY: The dogs in our village just ran about . . . they were everyone's, no one really owned them. *(Suddenly.)* Hang on!

SAM: What is it?

BOG BOY: The dogs . . . I haven't thought about them for — for a long time. I'm trying to remember, see. It's been so long, I forget, and I don't want to — I want to try and remember.

(Silence.)

SAM: Dad chose him for me, but he was mine. For my birthday when I was seven. I decided his name and fed him and everything.

BOG BOY: He had a name?

SAM: Course. Had it written on his collar.

BOG BOY: What was it?

SAM: It's embarrassing.

BOG BOY: Tell me.

SAM: No, you might laugh.

BOG BOY: I could do with a laugh, come on.

SAM: Smelly — his name was Smelly.

BOG BOY: What's wrong with that?

SAM: Most people think it's stupid. *(Silence.)* How come you talk like normal? How come you don't sound like Shakespeare or someone?

BOG BOY: Who's Shakespeare?

SAM: How come you don't say thee and thou and speak all ancient?

BOG BOY: You're not the only school to come here, you know. Day in, day out they come tramping through here, staring at me, putting finger marks all over my case so I can't see out — here, can you rub that bit, look? That was you, that was — rub it so it's clean, ta. *(Slight pause.)* I hear it and I pick it up I s'pose . . . the language. Your language. Completely forgotten how I used to speak.

SAM: Do you talk to any of the others?

BOG BOY: I did once, but he told me to stop — something about voices in his head.

SAM: Who gave it to you?

BOG BOY: What?

SAM: The brooch — you said it was a present.

BOG BOY: Bran.

SAM: Bran?

✦   ✦   ✦

Sam settles down next to Bog Boy's case.

SAM: You know the girl with the long hair? The pretty one . . . she used to be my best friend. *(Pause.)* Used to. *(Silence.)* Are you listening? *(Silence.)* She was kissing Dan — that's what all the noise was about earlier. On the sofa in front of everyone. *(Silence. Sam tuts.)* Come on then. *(Silence. Irritated.)* Come on!

BOG BOY: What?

SAM: *(Surprised.)* Oh —

BOG BOY: Come on what?

SAM: *(Meek.)* Say something.

BOG BOY: Like what?

SAM: *(Annoyed.)* How come you never speak when the others are here?

BOG BOY: You're special.

SAM: *(Embarrassed.)* Shut up!
    (Pause.)

BOG BOY: I can't see what you like about him, anyway.

SAM: Who?

BOG BOY: That boyfriend of yours.

SAM: He's not my boyfriend, is he.

BOG BOY: What's so special about him?

SAM: He's got nice eyes.

BOG BOY: Girls always say that about boys — *("Girlie" voice.)* "He's got lovely eyes!"

SAM: He has! And he's funny. Everyone likes him.

BOG BOY: Marks out of ten?

SAM: Ten, definitely. How do you know about marks out of ten?

BOG BOY: I'm not deaf, am I. I might be dead, but I'm not deaf.

SAM: Oh. *(Remembering how the others tried to make her kiss Bog Boy, Sam is embarrassed.)*

BOG BOY: *Bran* had lovely eyes.

SAM: What color?

BOG BOY: Blue.

SAM: So are Dan's.

BOG BOY: The rest of our village had brown eyes, but hers were
blue.

(Silence.)

SAM: Was she your girlfriend?

BOG BOY: My true love.

SAM: Oh. *(Pause.)* I don't love Dan. Like. A lot. But not love —
I'm too young.

BOG BOY: How can you be too young to love someone?

(Sam shrugs.)

SAM: It's what my mum says. Says I'm lucky not to love —
they'll only break your heart. *(Slight pause.)* My dad left
us. He's got another family. *(Slight pause.)* Where is she?

BOG BOY: Who?

SAM: Bran. Funny name . . . All Bran's what Dad used to have
for breakfast. Where is she?

BOG BOY: Bran means "raven." Why did your lot have to separate us? They left her behind. It wouldn't be so bad for
me if she was here too.

SAM: Tell me what she was like.

BOG BOY: Blue eyes.

SAM: What else?

BOG BOY: Black hair. Like a raven. *(Slight pause.)* I can't remember anything else! *(Upset.)* It's too long ago! I've forgotten
everything! Everything except the end, what happened at
the end.

SAM: What did happen?

BOG BOY: Stabbed.

SAM: You were?

BOG BOY: Fifteen times in the back and neck. They don't tell you
that bit, do they? You can see all the holes in my cloak
where the dagger went in.

SAM: Who stabbed you?

BOG BOY: Stabbed, then strangled, then drowned. But I still wasn't dead so they poisoned me.

SAM: Did it hurt?

(Bog Boy looks at her and pulls a face as if to say "Stupid question." There is a silence between them.)

BOG BOY: I knew it would. Sometimes pain's so — sharp, though . . . you can't feel it. You stop feeling. See Mother — crying. Can't look, can't stand. Falling. Both of us. See her cheek in the mud, others — Dad — help her up. Bran, on the ground . . . hair, sticky. Her blood and mine mingling, soaking in.

SAM: *(Hesitant.)* Did Bran die too?

BOG BOY: Didn't tell her I was scared. She knew it, but she wasn't scared, so I couldn't say how I . . . I couldn't tell her. We used to tell each other everything. Her so strong it made me weak. I didn't want to die. *(Pause.)* Must be why it took them so long. *(He shivers.)* I'm cold. *(Silence.)* Poison was worst. Sick and sick, over and over. Hard like iron through my whole body, tight, hard. Tightening. *(He shudders.)* Like others before me . . . every year when Spring comes. And one of the dogs once, when it ate some white berries . . . the sounds it made, coming out of my throat.

SAM: *(Whispers.)* That's horrible.

BOG BOY: After, when it was all over . . . *(He hesitates.)*

SAM: What? Tell me.

BOG BOY: All curled up soft in the dark at last. Like lying amongst the dogs asleep. And Bran's there. Warm. Can't feel where my body ends and the bog begins. Have you had that feeling? It's to do with the temperature . . . when you're the same temperature as the stuff around you. Now everything feels cold, the smallest sound or movement makes me — *(He shivers.)*

SAM: *(Gentle.)* Do you need me to talk quieter?

BOG BOY: It's all right, I like your voice. *(Silence. Quiet.)* We
were the sacrifice.

SAM: You and Bran.

(Silence.)

BOG BOY: Together. It was a noble death, they said. That's what
they told us. *(Grim.)* Didn't feel very noble.

The Honorable Urashima Taro
Coleman A. Jennings

This classic Japanese folktale tells of a young fisherman, Urashima Taro, who saves a wise old sea turtle from hunters. In reward, the turtle carries the young man to a wondrous undersea kingdom, where the fisherman is crowned a prince. In time, though, the fisherman must decide whether to remain in his new world and never grow old, or return to the world from which he came.

Five Males (and one nonspeaking part)

In the opening scene of this play, three young boys run onto a beach to discover a large sea turtle washed ashore. Shortly Taro and his little boy arrive and confront the boys, who have been taunting the turtle.

✦ ✦ ✦

Long ago. The shore of Shikoku, an island of Japan, near a little fishing village and the mountains and valleys of the ocean depths. Japanese music is playing as the audience enters the theater. There is no curtain, only screens upstage, painted to suggest a beach locale. As the house-lights dim, the Japanese music cross-fades to ocean sounds. The Turtle is "washed" ashore, settles at stage center, his back to the audience. The Three Boys run on stage, excited about going to the beach.

BOY THREE: The boats will be back soon!
BOY ONE: Hurry!
BOY TWO: I'll race you to the water!
BOY THREE: Look!

BOY TWO: Look what's on the beach! *(The Boys gather around the Turtle.)*

BOY ONE: I wonder how long he's been here?

BOY THREE: He must have been washed ashore.

BOY TWO: Look, how big he is!

BOY ONE: Yes, he is.

BOY THREE: Let's play with him.

BOY TWO: Watch out!

BOY ONE: Hit him!

BOY THREE: Let's take him to the village.

BOY ONE: No. No.

BOY TWO: *(Picking up a stick.)* Let me hit him!

BOY ONE: Make him stick out his head.

BOY TWO: Watch out, he'll bite you!

BOY THREE: How old is he?

BOY TWO: Who cares?

BOY ONE: Let's kill him.

BOY THREE: No, just turn him on his back.

BOY TWO: Wait! Here comes a boat.

BOY ONE: Who is it?

BOY THREE: It looks like Urashima Taro.

BOY ONE: It is Taro!

BOY THREE: *(Starting to leave.)* Let's go!

BOY TWO: Wait. I'm not afraid of Urashima Taro.

BOY THREE: But he will be angry with us!

BOY TWO: It's none of his business what we do. Who cares what he says?

BOY ONE: Does Taro own the sea or the beach?

BOY TWO: No. No!

BOY THREE: No, but he does care for the animals and sea creatures!

(Taro and his son, Kimo, are now near the shore.)

BOY TWO: If he is so kind to sea creatures, why does he catch fish every day?

BOY THREE: He catches fish for his family to sell in the market-place.

(Taro and Kimo leave their imaginary boat in the shallow water and approach the boys.)

TARO: Boys, what are you doing?

BOY TWO: Nothing.

TARO: What do you have there?

BOY TWO: A turtle we found on the beach!

TARO: But, what are you doing with it?

BOY ONE: Nothing. Just playing!

TARO: You have a strange way of playing. Why are you so cruel?

BOY TWO: We can do whatever we like! We found him. He's ours now.

TARO: *(Crossing to the Turtle.)* The turtle belongs to the sea.

BOY TWO: He should stay in the ocean if he doesn't want to be caught. He belongs to us, and we can kill him, if we want.

TARO: Why would you be so unkind to a poor creature?

BOY ONE: Look at your baskets! You catch and kill fish every day. Why shouldn't we kill an old turtle?

TARO: It is right to take the turtle if you are hungry, but you are teasing and hurting him.

BOY ONE: Look at him; he's old. Who cares if he lives?

TARO: You needn't kill him just because he is old. Think what a wonder it is to live so long — maybe even as long as three men!

BOY THREE: Yes, let's *not* kill him.

TARO: You do not need the turtle for food. Let's make a trade. We will give you some fish for him. Kimo, the fish. *(Kimo brings a small net of fish to Taro.)*

BOY ONE: We could use the fish.

BOY TWO: Why are you listening to him?

BOY ONE: We will do what we please. Leave us alone.

BOY TWO: Move out of the way!

(As the argument builds, Boy Two attempts to strike the

Turtle with the stick. Boy Three grabs his arm and holds him.)

TARO: *(As he covers the Turtle with his body.)* Wait! You must not kill him!

BOY TWO: Get away! He belongs to us!

TARO: *(Angrily.)* He belongs to no one. Now go home. *(Pause, then firmly, but kindly.)* Boys! Here are fish for your family. *(Pause.)* Go on. *(Boy Two puts the stick down and exits with Boy One, without accepting any fish. Boy Three remains with Taro and Kimo.)*

BOY THREE: I'm sorry. I hadn't meant to be so cruel. *(Turns to leave.)*

KIMO: I wonder how deeply he can swim.

BOY THREE: Maybe he's been on this beach before.

TARO: Let's help him return to his home.

KIMO: *(As they help the Turtle into the "water.")* He *is* big. *(Note: The actors never touch the Turtle. Keeping their hands approximately six inches from him, they create a stylized effect of grabbing the shell. The Turtle retains complete freedom of movement.)*

TARO: Yes, my son, and he is handsome, too. Now he will be free. Be on your way, ancient one!

KIMO AND BOY THREE: *(To the Turtle as he begins to exit into the sea.)* Good-bye.

TARO: *(As Boy Three starts to exit, calling him back.)* Wait. *(Offering him some fish.)* Take these to your family.

BOY THREE: All of these?

TARO: Take them, and go along.

BOY THREE: Thank you for the fish. Good-bye, Kimo. Good-bye, Urashima Taro.

TARO AND KIMO: Good-bye.

Hula Heart
Velina Hasu Houston

Seven-year-old Sean "Kilo" Hauptmann, a multiethnic boy from Hawaii, moves to Southern California with his family, where he attempts to pursue his love of the popular Polynesian dance, the hula. Sean befriends Caleb, another boy who shares like traditions, but most of his new mainland acquaintances mock them. In the clash of pop culture and native traditions, Sean learns much about himself and his place in life.

Three Males and One Female

In the first scene below, Sean, who has beeen practicing hula and shaking bamboo rattles (*pu'ili*), encounters Julian, one of his new mainland classmates. Sean tries to explain the island traditions. In the second scene, Sean meets Caleb, another new classmate with whom he has more in common than not. The last scene brings Sean back in contact with Julian, who still is not ready to accept the island ways. (Note: You may want to research Hawaiian musical instruments and vocabulary.)

✦ ✦ ✦

JULIAN: What you doing, dude?

SEAN: *(Grabs his* pu'ili *and conceals them behind his back.)* Nothing!

JULIAN: Yeah? Don't you know this is a basketball court?

SEAN: Uh . . . I was just, ah, fooling around.

JULIAN: You're that new kid from Hawaii, huh? That loud shirt gives it away.

SEAN: It's an aloha shirt!

JULIAN: But it's got flowers on it, in case you haven't noticed. *Big, loud* flowers. Boys don't wear flowers.

SEAN: It's dress-up. My mom made me wear it for school!

JULIAN: Oh, your mommy made you!

SEAN: *(Aside.)* Thanks, Mom! *(To Julian.)* Yeah. So what?

JULIAN: Sixth graders don't like mama's boys.

SEAN: Wow! You're a sixth grader, yeah?

JULIAN: I'm *the* sixth grader, the big J. You don't look Hawaiian to me, though. You look like one of us.

SEAN: *(Proudly.)* I'm chop suey! A little Hawaiian, Japanese, Chinese, Portuguese, Puerto Rican, German, Eng —

JULIAN: *(Cuts him off.)* Whoa! Too much to remember! I'll just call you Hawaiian Bud. So, H.B., break it down for me. What kinda junk were you just doing like you got no sense?

SEAN: For your information, it's not junk. It's *hula.*

JULIAN: Hula?! *(Laughing uncontrollably.)* Man, don't tell me you put on those grass skirts and coconut shells and shake your hips to that silly kinda music!

(Lights suddenly darken as figment of Julian's imagination emerges: corny music fades in and hula dancer [Caleb] wearing wild wig, makeup, coconut-shell halter, and wild grass skirt shimmies across stage. Exit dancer, music fading out concurrently.)

JULIAN: The sixth graders'll laugh you right outta school if they see you like that, H.B.

SEAN: In Honolulu, I belonged to a *halau.*

JULIAN: A what?

SEAN: A school for hula.

JULIAN: You went to school to be a coconut girl?!

SEAN: Lots of guys do hula! Coconuts are Tahitian style — for girls! Not for *keika kane!*

JULIAN: "Cake" what? Speak English!

SEAN: What do you know about hula anyway? You don't know anything, yeah.

JULIAN: Hey, just trying to do you a favor, H.B. You're in Southern California now — the U.S. of A. — and —

SEAN: Hawaii is part of the United States, too!

JULIAN: Oh, yeah. Kinda forget that sometimes. Anyway, take my word for it. You don't want a hard time, don't be different. Kids'll say, "You can't play ball with us, Aloha Girl!"

SEAN: Well, what should I do?

(Julian passes ball challengingly to Sean, who tries to rise to the occasion, but stumbles because of his thongs.)

JULIAN: Basketball: something respectable, little man. But not in those flip-flops! Whatcha wearing flip-flops to school for, H.B.? Get yourself some sneakers, OK?

SEAN: We wear slippers all the time in Hawaii, yeah.

JULIAN: You're driving me crazy with that "yeah" stuff! Does every sentence have to end with "yeah"? Is that a Hawaiian thing?

SEAN: No, everbody in Hawaii does it, not just Hawaiians.

JULIAN: But isn't everybody in Hawaii Hawaiian?

SEAN: No! There's *haoles* — white people — and there's local people. All mixed up, *bra*.

JULIAN: Bra! Talk about mixed up! A bra's something girls wear.

SEAN: *(To audience.)* Jeez, they don't understand English here!

JULIAN: So take if from me: you're the H.B., period. Put those overgrown chopsticks in your bag. Don't slouch. Trash the wack shirt. And then guess what?

SEAN: What?

JULIAN: You're *Kapow!*

(Julian teaches Sean special handshake as two bond.)

SEAN: Kapow!

(Blackout.)

✦ ✦ ✦

Sean awkwardly tries to spin basketball on his finger; he can't do it. It rolls offstage and he's about to retrieve it when it is returned by friendly Caleb Schoenberg. Caleb tosses ball back and forth between his palms and then deftly passes it between his legs before passing it to Sean.

SEAN: Thanks. Watch this! *(Tries to spin ball on his finger, succeeds.)* Kapow!

CALEB: What's that mean: kapow?

SEAN: Just something cool my best friend taught me.

CALEB: Nah. For real? What's that? What does it mean?
(Caleb exits momentarily. Sean addresses audience with his pu'ili *up as antenna.)*

SEAN: I smell another alien!
(Sean quickly puts the pu'ili *back into his bag. Caleb returns with a gym bag. Caleb's* pu'ili *accidently falls out and he tries to stuff them back in, but Sean gasps and picks them up.)*

SEAN: Why do you have these?

CALEB: Uh . . . they're monster teeth! *(Holds them up to his mouth and makes ferocious face. Both boys laugh hard.)*

SEAN: *(Aside to audience.)* I like this kid!

CALEB: They're for a kind of . . . club I belong to. They're called —

SEAN AND CALEB: *Pu'ili!*
(Both pull out their pu'ili *as weapons and play-fight, finally electrocuting each other. Each dies a dramatic death. Pause. Sean pops up his head.)*

SEAN: Hey, what's your name?

CALEB: I'm Caleb.

SEAN: I'm Sean. We moved in across the street.

CALEB: How come you know about *pu'ili?*

SEAN: I belonged to a *halau* in Honolulu.

CALEB: Hey, my mom's from Hawaii. We go there a lot. I belong to a *halau* here!

(The boys subconsciously slip into pidgin.)

SEAN: Wow, a Hawaiian *halau* in Southern California?

CALEB: Not just Hawaiian. It's got all kinda people in it. You wanna join? I can talk to my *kumu* about you. Her name's Auntie Ingrid, and she's real cool.

SEAN: But Caleb —

CALEB: You can call me Kala. It's short for Kamehanaokala, my Hawaiian name. It means warmth of the sun.

SEAN: Kala. That's nice. Kala, don't the kids at school give you a hard time for being interested in the hula?

CALEB: Who cares what they say? They play basketball and do hip-hop, I play basketball and do hula. What's the diff?

SEAN: I'm not very good at basketball, but I used to be real good at hula.

CALEB: How old are you?

SEAN: Seven. But I'll be eight in a couple of months!

CALEB: Perfect. I'm nine. You can be in my group in the *halau*. Come on.

SEAN: I have to ask my mom first. If I leave the yard, I'll get scoldings.

CALEB: OK. It's that gray house at the end of the block, so you'll be safe walking with me.

SEAN: You sure your *kumu* won't mind me coming?

CALEB: No. That's the magic of hula, yeah.

SEAN: The magic?

CALEB: You gotta share it!

SEAN: But what if some people don't care about it?

CALEB: You show 'em the hula in your heart, and they will. I love it. You love it. They'll love it, too.

SEAN: You think?

CALEB: That's the magic!

(Lights begin to fade out as . . .)

SEAN: *(Stage whisper.)* . . . the magic . . . !

(As lights cross-fade, Sean and Caleb run, taking turns chas-

ing each other, using pu'ili *in different comic ways. En route, Caleb picks up bag of his own hula instruments.)*

SEAN: My mom said it's OK!

CALEB: This is gonna be fun! We can dance together in the fall concert!

SEAN: Concert?

CALEB: It's a really big deal, yeah. We work hard all year long to show our stuff. All kinda people come and see how great hula is.

SEAN: Like you said, we share what we love.

CALEB: And everybody understands each other a little better, yeah.

SEAN: Yeah!

(Lights come to rest on the halau. Contemporary Hawaiian music plays softly in background. Sean and Caleb survey hula instruments of the halau with respect: pu'ili, 'ili'ili, uili, 'ulili, ipu, 'uli'uli, puniu *and* ka, *and* pa'hu.*)*

SEAN: Gee, I feel like I'm back home! So what hula are you working on now?

CALEB: Lots. My favorite is "Hole Waimea." *(Does small piece of hula, "Hole Waimea.")* Do you know that one?

SEAN: Kinda.

(Boys slip into pidgin without noticing.)

CALEB: Well, either you do or you don't.

SEAN: I did it a long time ago. I kinda remember the words.

CALEB: If you join our *halau*, you'll work on that 'cause the keiki kane will perform it in our fall concert right before Thanksgiving.

SEAN: Gee, that's only three months to learn it.

CALEB: You've been in a *halau* before. You'll be OK. But we don't just learn our hula, we live them. We gotta be that good 'cause the concert's our one big chance a year to pass on the hula.

SEAN: That's a whole lotta pressure.

CALEB: It's nothing as long as the whole *halau* sticks together. Especially our group 'cause there's not too many boys, not like in Honolulu. So you with me, yeah.

SEAN: Oh, yeah.

CALEB: You wanna learn all the secret uses of the hula instruments? Watch, OK? But I gotta use mine 'cause Kumu's are sacred. Don't ever mess with her stuff!

(Caleb with a fake regal accent holds his 'ulili over his head, and Sean joins in.)

SEAN AND CALEB: Ancient Hawaiian headdress!

CALEB: *(Fake regal accent as he covers his nostrils with his 'ili'ili.)* Ancient Hawaiian nose covers made of dried dog poo!

(Boys mimic pig behavior just as Auntie Ingrid enters. She screams, jaws agape, and then appears comically faint at their behavior.)

AUNTIE INGRID: Please tell me that I do not see my *keiki kane* disgracing the sacred instruments of hula!

CALEB: No, no! These are mine, Kumu! I would never touch yours! Never!

(Sean and Caleb immediately set down instruments and look ashamed.)

SEAN: Sorry!

CALEB: It was, uh, just a game!

AUNTIE INGRID: Hula is not a game. If you want to play a game, go to the playground and climb monkey bars. When you are ready for hula, respect the instruments, the *halau*, and everything else in it. Including yourselves.

SEAN: Yes, ma'am.

CALEB: Yes, Kumu.

AUNTIE INGRID: Where, after all, are your hula hearts? It certainly breaks mine to see these instruments being used in such ways! Promise me you'll never, ever do this again.

SEAN AND CALEB: Never!

CALEB: *(Aside to Sean.)* Not when she's watching anyway!

SEAN: *(Aside to audience.)* Cool!

(Boys giggle; sharp glance from Kumu makes them cease quickly. Pleased, she beams.)

AUNTIE INGRID: Good! Shall we start anew now that we've had a lesson in manners?

CALEB: *Aloha kaua e kumu.*

AUNTIE INGRID: *Aloha kaua e,* Kamehanaokala.

SEAN: *Aloha,* Auntie Ingrid.

AUNTIE INGRID: *Aloha kaua e,* Kilohoku. But you can say "aloha kaua" like Kala, then you honor yourself, too, in the beauty, the embrace of *aloha.* Do you know what the embrace of *aloha* is?

SEAN: *(Wrinkles his brow in thought.)* Well . . .

+ + +

At school, Sean attempts hula and a mele *(song), "A Ka Luna o'Kilauea." His open lunch box is beside him. He looks up to see someone standing over him.*

SEAN: Oh, hi, Miss Cook. Yeah, I belong to a *halau,* a hula school. Do it at home? For my safety? Yeah . . . I guess I understand. Uh, thanks for protecting me. *(He watches her exit. Before he can resume his hula practice, he looks up as if in response to a friendly encounter.)* Yeah, I'm Sean, friend of the Big J. He told you about me, huh? We're real tight, yeah. We just saw each other and, ya know — kapow — we hit it off just like that! *(Persona fades, and Sean basks in glory. To audience.)* Wow! The Big J's tellin' people I'm his buddy! Talk about cool! *(Sean begins to practice hula and is startled by Julian's appearance.)*

JULIAN: Whoa, whoa. H.B., I thought we were clear on this hula stuff. And you're still wearing flip-flops! Get with the program — now — or you're not hanging with me.

SEAN: B-b-but I thought we were, ya know, best friends . . .

JULIAN: What?! I never said that! You're a squirt, H.B. OK, I guess you can say you're my little buddy, but don't get aheada yourself.

SEAN: Right! Sorry! Cool shades, Big J!

JULIAN: By the way, you're horning in on my territory big time.

SEAN: Your territory?

JULIAN: Yeah. On Fridays, I always eat lunch here in the very spot you're sitting in, so *move*.

(Sean quickly moves and starts to pack his lunch, but Julian quickly puts his hand on lunch.)

JULIAN: Penalty! I get whatever I want from your lunch box. Whatcha got?

SEAN: Spam *musubi*.

JULIAN: What?! Moose meat?

SEAN: Spam *musubi*. Kinda like a rice ball with a big slab of Spam on top, wrapped up with seaweed.

JULIAN: That's disgusting, man! Got anything American in there?

SEAN: Ate everything else.

(Julian eats a musubi — *and likes it.)*

JULIAN: Say, not bad! *(Eats another.)*

SEAN: Hey, you said one!

(Julian gives him menacing glance; Sean backs down.)

JULIAN: You know how to surf?

SEAN: Kinda. I — I mean . . . sure!

JULIAN: Maybe I'll teach you. Yeah. We'll hit some waves after school — but gotta bring more of this moose meat.

SEAN: But I'm s'posed to go to hula practice. Nah, I'll ask my mom if I can go with you.

JULIAN: Cool. My mom'll drive us. Maybe I'll show you a secret place.

SEAN: Wow! Thanks!

(Julian whips shades back over his hair, but they fall. Sean quickly picks up shades and hands them to Julian.)

JULIAN: Cool. So have your mom drop you off at my house. Here's the address. It's close.

(Julian grabs last musubi; Sean is about to protest, but stops. Julian starts to chew away. Laka appears and stands behind him, concentrating all her energy on him. His chewing grows difficult, and his face contorts as if there's a bad taste in his mouth. Laka smiles and exits.)

SEAN: Is something wrong, Big J?

(Julian spits out food, a rubber frog. He freaks out, and his shades fall again.)

JULIAN: What the — ! ! !

SEAN: I didn't do it! Honest!

JULIAN: I don't eat raw frog, OK?

SEAN: OK! Sorry! *(Aside to audience.)* How'd that happen anyway?

JULIAN: You get one more chance to enter the kingdom of cool, but be ready to earn it!

(Sean nods enthusiastically as Julian exits. Lights cross-fade to spotlight into which Sean enters. "Mom" music plays as pile of clothes/shoes gets tossed into light, and Sean puts them on.)

SEAN: *(Re: music.)* Ouch! Mom, turn that stuff back! *(Re: ensemble.)* How much these shoes cost? Whoa! These clothes aren't weird, Mom. They're cool! Like the Big J! *(Mom messes with his hair.)* No, Mom! I gotta wear my hair like this. Check out these sunglasses, Mom. Cool! Now I'm reeeaaaaddddy!

The Invisible Man
Len Jenkins

Adapted from the H.G. Wells story and set in the 1950s, Jack Griffin — face bandaged — is living in an old motel near a nuclear power plant. He befriends Jim, a small boy, whose father had been the caretaker of the plant until his recent death. In the course of serving as the boy's "father figure," Jack reveals that he must wear bandages because a nuclear accident at the plant caused him to become invisible. But is this the truth? In the process of answering this question, Jim is forced to make difficult decisions.

Two Males

In the following scene, Jim, who is playing Martian Invader at an old drive-in movie lot, encoutner Griffin, the Invisible Man, for the first time.

✦ ✦ ✦

Drive-in movie theater. Some snow is still on ground. A raised stage; large, tattered screen. In front of stage is children's playground: seesaw, other beat-up playground equipment. Leaning against stage is Jim's bike. Jim himself is onstage wearing his Mars invader mask. He's using drive-in speaker for microphone.

JIM: Calling Captain Cappy! Calling Captain Cappy! We're about fifty kilomiles from the Martian Canal City, and coming in fast. What are your orders? *(Holding speaker to ear, listening, then back to mouth.)* Right, Captain. Should we hold our fire till we talk to the Martians?

(Jim holds speaker to ear. From behind movie screen, Griffin appears, head still bandaged, showing only pink nose and blue-tinted glasses. He wears huge scarf and black fedora.)

GRIFFIN: Shoot first, ask questions later.

JIM: *(Turns, surprised and frightened, lifting off mask.)* Hey, what are you doing out here?

GRIFFIN: Sorry I scared you. Ron told me about this place. I thought I'd take a look. I been meaning to send for one of those Mars invaders masks, myself.

JIM: They're not for grown-ups.

GRIFFIN: Sometimes grown-ups need hideouts, too. *(Imitating Captain Cappy.)* "The best hideout ever! Magic forehead vision lets you see out, but nobody sees in." A lot of scientists like "Space Patrol." Try your bike?

(Griffin hops on, rides bike in among playground equipment, tooting horn, Jim comes down offstage.)

JIM: Jack? What kind of science do you do? My dad was an engineer.

GRIFFIN: I'm no engineer, Jim. I'm a . . . an atomic power specialist. *(Hops off bike, leans it against stage.)* I used to work at the Glowville Nuclear Reactor, right up the road.

JIM: Glowville! I'd love to work there someday.

GRIFFIN: I quit. The other scientists tried to steal from me.

JIM: Steal? Steal what?

GRIFFIN: My discoveries. The results of years of research. Now, when I record my experiments in my notebooks, it's all in my own private code. Can you keep a secret, Jim?

JIM: I think so.

GRIFFIN: They're still after me — those thieves of science. They'll do anything to get their dirty hands on my notebooks. Valuable research. It's why I came to this quiet place, hoping they'd never find me here, and I could work in peace. I need someone to be my lookout, Jim — to watch for those thieving rats. Human slime. I'll pay you. If any strangers come near the inn, you run back and tell me.

JIM: I don't know, Jack. I've got a lot of stuff to do around the —

GRIFFIN: *(Holding out money.)* Here's an advance on your salary.

JIM: Twenty dollars!

GRIFFIN: Buy yourself a portable radio, so you'll have some company when you watch out there on the road. Take it.

JIM: Mom wouldn't like it if I spent money on something like that.

GRIFFIN: Then don't tell her.

JIM: *(Can't resist and takes cash.)* Jack, you've got yourself a lookout!

GRIFFIN: Watch out for Santa Claus.

JIM: Who?

GRIFFIN: A poison Santa Claus. A white beard, and long white hair. Walks with a cane. Professor Cosmo Gibson, my ex-boss at the atomic power plant. He'll say he's my friend, that he's trying to help me. Lies. He's a very dangerous man, Jim.

JIM: He won't sneak by me!

GRIFFIN: Jim, it makes me feel a lot safer to have you helping me. Tomorrow, all my equipment arrives! Chemical, radiological, biological. Once it's all set up in the parlor, work can begin. I have high hopes, Jim. High hopes!

(Griffin exits. Putting on space patrol Mars invader mask, Jim goes on small stage. Using speaker as ray gun, he steps forward boldly.)

JIM: Ready, space patrollers! This is Jim Winters, look out! Follow me! And if you see any Martians — shoot first and ask questions later!

(Cross-fade to parlor, next day. Parlor has become chemical laboratory with pile of bedding in one corner indicating someone lives there. On dining table are bubbling retorts, Bunsen burners, racks of test tubes, radiation monitors, and lead-lined boxes with glove inserts for working

with radioactive material. Griffin, in bandages and wear-
ing floor-length bathrobe, scarf, and blue-tinted glasses, is
busy near cat's cage. Attached to cage are electrical wiring,
food tubes, and meters. Griffin takes off one glove, leaving
it at far end of table, pours green liquid from beaker into
opaque bottle on side of cat's cage. He appears to have no
hand, and beaker rises, pours, and empties as if handled by
hand that isn't there. A knock at door. Griffin, preoccupied,
doesn't hear it. Jim enters, hesitantly.)

JIM: Uh, Mr. Griffin? Can I come in? Jack?

GRIFFIN: *(Jumps in fright, hides his seemingly empty sleeve*
behind him.) Get out! I told you to knock! Can't you understand English, you little idiot! Knock means knock!

JIM: I did knock! You didn't hear me. I figured you were doing
research, I thought —

GRIFFIN: You thought! Don't think! Just do what I tell you!

JIM: Do you want me to go?
(Pause.)

GRIFFIN: I'm sorry, Jim. When I'm involved in my work, I get
tense and . . . you surprised me. I didn't mean to yell at you.

JIM: That's OK. I was just hoping I could tune in "Space Patrol."
It comes on pretty soon.

GRIFFIN: Sure, I'd like to listen, myself. Go ahead, turn on the
radio. I've got to finish this procedure.
(Griffin works, still hiding his invisible hand, trying dis-
creetly to retrieve glove from table. Jim picks up radiation
meter and flips on switch. It begins to tick loudly, and red
light flashes. Surprised and frightened, Jim holds it out at
arm's length, toward Griffin. Warning siren wails.)

JIM: Help! Jack! This thing's goin' crazy!

GRIFFIN: Give me that, you fool! *(Grabs meter and flips switch*
off, forgetting he's wearing one glove.)

JIM: Sorry! I didn't realize . . . Oh, my Lord! What happened
to your hand?

GRIFFIN: *(Look down, realizing that Jim sees that he has no hand.)* I . . . uh . . . I . . . didn't want to tell you, Jim. In the accident when my face was injured — I also lost an arm. I've got a prosthesis — a wooden arm I use to look normal. I take if off sometimes when I'm working.

JIM: Oh.

GRIFFIN: Now this radiation meter probably picked up a trace amount of tri-oxy-neuro-chromo-ethanol in my jacket fibers.

JIM: *(Continues to stare at Griffin's invisible hand and seemingly empty sleeve.)* If you took off your wooden arm, how come your sleeve is still standing up like that? How come you could grab the radiation meter with a hand that isn't there?

GRIFFIN: You're a bright boy, Jim. I like that. I'm going to show you what my work is all about. I have to. You've seen too much already. Take off my other glove.

(Griffin holds out gloved hand to Jim, who pulls glove off. Jim stares, open-mouthed.)

GRIFFIN: I hope you can keep an important scientific secret — and be a true friend. *(Suddenly pulls nose off and hands it to Jim.)*

JIM: My God! Your nose!

(Griffin takes off blue-tinted glasses, begins to unwind bandages from around his head.)

Your eyes — they're just holes . . .

GRIFFIN: *(Tosses unwound bandages to floor. He is without visible hands and head.)* Happy Halloween, Jim!

JIM: I . . . uh . . . you're . . .

GRIFFIN: I'm an invisible man.

JIM: But you're . . . you're . . .

GRIFFIN: Transparent.

JIM: You're — an invisible man!

GRIFFIN: Bingo!

The King of Ireland's Son
Paula Wing

This beloved Celtic folktale is brought to fresh light with great humor and adventure when an enchanted bird calls Sean the Red to free his sister from an ancient prison. On his way, Sean meets a loyal friend, a powerful giant, a captivating fairy, and a monstrous sea serpent, the Urfeist. As Sean battles the sea serpent, the Princess Finola appears, and Sean discovers that destiny has something more in store for him.

Two Males

In the scene that follows, Sean stumbles over a little green bush that turns out to be a little green man — a leprechaun! At first there is a tussle, but soon the little man and Sean are off to find the Giant who captured the King of Ireland's daughter.

SEAN: *(To himself.)* The Druid never said, "Don't give it away." I had to give it. Didn't I? I have to keep my head about me. Eejit! Where's my Bird anyway? He's meant to advise me and he's nowhere to be found. It's not fair. Has he deserted me maybe because I needed that fiver to ransom my sister? Maybe? Aaugh! I hate all this thinking! Why can't I just fight? *(He starts walking and trips over a small green bush.)*
THE BUSH: *Musha,* there's no call for that.
SEAN: Who's there?
(The bush is actually a Little Green Man who now stands up, affronted.)
THE LITTLE GREEN MAN: You young hooligan! I'm bruised entirely!

SEAN: A leprechaun!

THE LITTLE GREEN MAN: Where?

SEAN: You're not a leprechaun?

THE LITTLE GREEN MAN: Me? Are you daft, man?

SEAN: *(Draws his sword.)* Well what are you then? Who are you? Out with it or I'll carve out your voice box and spear your name on the tip of me sword.

THE LITTLE GREEN MAN: *(Screams wildly.)* Don't kill me, bejeez! Is it money I owe you?

SEAN: Tell me everything you know about the Giant who captured the King of Ireland's daughter or I'll —

THE LITTLE GREEN MAN: *(Babbling.)* Ireland? What d'ye — I don't — how could I — the King of —

SEAN: Speak!

THE LITTLE GREEN MAN: Help!

SEAN: I'll run you through. I'm not afraid of anything at all at all.

THE LITTLE GREEN MAN: I am. I am! Pure terrified! *(Runs back and forth wildly, squawking with panic.)*

SEAN: Don't move! Why are you moving? I told you not to move.

(With a groaning cry of battle Sean rushes at The Little Green Man as if to run him through, and somehow in the tussle the sword comes right out of Sean's hand. The Little Green Man snatches it up.)

THE LITTLE GREEN MAN: Me nerves are in bits. That's as close to death as I — *(He stops himself and looks around, as though he'd just awakened.)* Be the mortal day!

SEAN: Go on and kill me. I deserve to die!

THE LITTLE GREEN MAN: Too much work, laddie. And besides, that Crane of yours, he wouldn't —

SEAN: You saw my Bird? Where is he? Show me where he went?

THE LITTLE GREEN MAN: Oh, I couldn't tell you where he was

now at all at all. *(He comes upon a bun in his pocket.)* Nourishment! Would you ever share it with me?

SEAN: No, I have to find my Bird. Oh. Wait! Is that a gift? The bun?

THE LITTLE GREEN MAN: We won't know 'til we taste it. Are you hungry?

SEAN: I am.

THE LITTLE GREEN MAN: I always think better after I've supped. We'll go looking for your Crane later.

SEAN: No "we" won't, sir. I'll be lookin' for my Bird meself, thank you very much.

THE LITTLE GREEN MAN: Really. Why?

SEAN: Why? Be cripes, I have to. It's my destiny.

THE LITTLE GREEN MAN: Nobody does anything alone in this world, my son. Except die.

SEAN: The heroes do. Cuchulainn and Fionn MacCumhaill do, surely.

THE LITTLE GREEN MAN: And you're a hero yourself, are you?

SEAN: I am.

THE LITTLE GREEN MAN: *(Half to himself.)* Saints preserve us. *(Regarding his bun.)* What's more mairvellocious than a bite of sustenance, I ask you? When you think of it, our stomachs are like heaven for food. My teeth are this bun's pearly gates.

SEAN: Take a gander at this. *(He executes an extremely awkward jump/leap move.)*

THE LITTLE GREEN MAN: And what was that now?

SEAN: My salmon leap.

THE LITTLE GREEN MAN: Your salmon leap?

SEAN: Just like Cuchulainn's when he fought the — what? What's so funny?

THE LITTLE GREEN MAN: "Just like Cuchulainn." It's enough to make a fish laugh.

SEAN: The *Shanachies* are going to sing ballads about it 'til the end of time. Then you'll be laughing out the other side of your mouth!

THE LITTLE GREEN MAN: Oh, you're goin' to end the story famine all be yourself, is it?

SEAN: I am. It's my *Diachbha*.

THE LITTLE GREEN MAN: Bejeez, it tires me out just thinkin' about it.

SEAN: I can't stand here talking all day. I have to find my Bird. Good luck to you so. Thanks for the bite. *(He nearly turns his back, then starts to back away.)*

THE LITTLE GREEN MAN: Here, wait. Ehm. Well. You wouldn't mind a little company, would you?

SEAN: I would. The Druid never said anything about anybody comin' with me so.

THE LITTLE GREEN MAN: Did he say somebody couldn't come with you?

SEAN: No.

THE LITTLE GREEN MAN: Then where's the harm in it?

SEAN: I'm going alone and there's an end.

THE LITTLE GREEN MAN: You'd turn your back on a poor wee brussels sprout of a fella like me?

SEAN: I didn't turn my back!

THE LITTLE GREEN MAN: That was the feeling of it. You wounded me, sure, and me after savin' your sorry life not five minutes ago.

SEAN: I didn't mean to — it's just that I —

THE LITTLE GREEN MAN: No harm done. I'll come with you and not another word spoken.

SEAN: No! It's my Bird and my destiny.

THE LITTLE GREEN MAN: I offer the lad the pleasure, the pure *gift* of my company, a thing most men would weep to get even the smell of and it's no, he says. Picture it!

SEAN: Wait, don't go. I — however did you know? It's not fair. *(After a moment.)* I have to fight all the battles.

THE LITTLE GREEN MAN: I take a dread oath to leave all the bloodshed to you. *(He starts off. Sean doesn't move.)* Ah, don't get a puss on, it's not worth it. I'm Shaking Head.

Pinocchio
Timothy Mason

Here is a delightful and charming adaptation of the Italian folk tale about Geppetto's little puppet boy, Pinocchio, who learns the value in truth and discovers the love that turns him into a real boy.

Two Males

In the first scene below, Pinocchio, at home in Geppetto's shop, studies his ABCs and prepares to head off to school. In the second scene, Geppetto, who has been searching for the lost Pinocchio, is reunited with his little wooden boy in the cavernous belly of a whale.

+ + +

Lights rise on Geppetto's workshop. A rainy morning. Pinocchio is alone, dressed in a little apron, sweeping the floor as he recites his ABCs.

PINOCCHIO: A, B, C, D, E, F, G, H . . . H . . . H . . . A, B, C, D, E, F, G, H . . . H . . .
(Pinocchio stops his sweeping, looks about to see that he is alone, then upends the broom and tries to balance it on the end of his finger. After several balances, wobbles, and falls, the broom falls against the mantel, knocking the clock to the floor with a crash and release of springs.)
GEPPETTO: *(Offstage.)* Pinocchio! I'm home!
(Pinocchio looks at the broken clock in dismay, then fervently resumes sweeping the floor. Geppetto enters,

clutching a small package; he is wet and shivering without his overcoat.)

PINOCCHIO: *(Rushing over to Geppetto.)* Papa! Papa! What comes after H, Papa?

GEPPETTO: I comes after H, you know *that!* But look, Pinocchio — you gonna learn your ABCs real good from now on. Look — a brand new spelling book!

PINOCCHIO: *(Hugging him.)* Oh, Papa! Now I can go to school just like all the other boys!

GEPPETTO: Sure you can, Pinocchio! To school!

(They dance happily for a moment.)

GEPPETTO: But, hey — Pinocchio — you aint gonna go to school with an apron on, are you?

(Pinocchio removes his apron and sets it on the bench.)

PINOCCHIO: Papa, where is your coat? It's cold and rainy outside.

GEPPETTO: Oh, I don't know . . . it was, uh . . . too hot. But don't worry about that, Pinocchio. It must be time for you to go to school, huh? Hey — what time *is* it, Pinocchio?

PINOCCHIO: *(Suddenly hanging his head in shame.)* I don't know.

GEPPETTO: *(Thinking he's embarrassed due to ignorance.)* Oh, that's all right, Pinocchio. I teach you to tell me . . . *(Geppetto turns toward the mantel and sees no clock. He looks at the floor, crouches, and picks up shattered pieces of the clock.)* Oh, oh. My old clock don't look too happy.

(Slight pause as Geppetto looks at Pinocchio, waiting for an explanation. Pinocchio offers none.)

GEPPETTO: Do you think Kitty might have broke the clock, Pinocchio?

PINOCCHIO: *(A thought.)* Kitty? Kitty *might* have. Maybe Kitty was playing and the clock fell down and broke, or . . .

(Pinocchio suddenly stops and taps his nose twice.)

GEPPETTO: What's the matter, Pinocchio? You nose itch?

PINOCCHIO: *(A slight pause.)* You know what, Papa?

GEPPETTO: No. What.

PINOCCHIO: It wasn't Kitty who done it.

GEPPETTO: Really?

PINOCCHIO: It was me. I seen the other boys; sometimes they balance a stick, and I tried it, and I'm sorry, Papa. I wish I didn't.

GEPPETTO: *(Hugging Pinocchio.)* Pinocchio — if this was my favorite clock, I don't care if it's broke. What's important is you didn't lie to me. You know, Pinocchio — lies, they just keep on growing. They ain't no good.

(The sound of schoolboys yelling in the street outside.)

GEPPETTO: But listen, the others boys is already on their way to school You go to, eh? Arrivederci.

PINOCCHIO: *(Starting off.)* Good-bye, Papa!

GEPPETTO: Oh, Pinocchio — when you come home tonight, I'll have a nice surprise for you.

PINOCCHIO: *(Waving.)* Arrivederci?

GEPPETTO: Ciao! *(Suddenly seeing spelling book on workbench.)* Pinocchio! You forgot your spelling book!

(Pinocchio rushes back, takes the book, and then hugs Geppetto.)

PINOCCHIO: I love you, Papa!

GEPPETTO: Ciao!

(Pinocchio runs out. Geppetto sighs and turns proudly to audience.)

GEPPETTO: That's Pinocchio. I made him. He's my son!

(Music in. Workshop shifts and Geppetto exits.)

✦ ✦ ✦

We hear the gentle lapping of water and dripping, reverberating as if in an enormous cave. Far upstage we see the faint glow of a lantern, which draws nearer. As it does so, it illumines the set: The lantern is hanging on a tiny boat that holds Geppetto. We are inside the belly of the whale:

Huge bluish-red riblike membranes surround the stage and stretch upstage to infinity. The distant sound of the whale's belch.

GEPPETTO: *(Listening.)* Thunder? No. No thunder here. No clouds. No sky. No days. No days in the belly of a whale. Only nights. Only one long night. *(He sits on a little stool, dejected.)* Oh, Pinocchio . . . where did you go? Where did you go, Pinocchio? *(He wipes away a tear.)* Ahh, Geppetto — how about something to eat? Whadda you gonna eat tonight, eh? How about . . . some fish? That sounds real good. Of course, I *could* have some fish, instead. Then again, I could have some fish. No, I've got it: some fish! *(Geppetto tosses a line over the upstage side of his boat.)* Come on, fishy. Come to Geppetto. Come on. *(A big tug on the line.)* Hey! What's this pulling so hard . . . *(Another tug. Geppetto looks over the edge of the boat.)* Hey — this fish got hands! *(He reaches down and pulls a hand over the side.)* Hands and . . . arms! *(Two arms hook themselves over the side; Geppetto reaches over and pulls. Pinocchio flies into the boat, looks up, sees Geppetto.)*

PINOCCHIO: *(Holding out his arms.)* Papa!

GEPPETTO: Pinocchio!

(They embrace.)

GEPPETTO: Pinocchio! Oh, Pinocchio . . . I never thought . . . oh, Pinocchio!

PINOCCHIO: Papa — how did you get here?

GEPPETTO: Pinocchio, I look for you *everywhere* . . . where did you go, Pinocchio? Where did you go?

PINOCCHIO: Oh, Papa — I met these two friends and they took me to Pigacci's Puppet Theater to get rich.

GEPPETTO: *I* went to the puppet show, but Signor Pigacci got real mad when I said your name, so I knowed you must have been there.

PINOCCHIO: Then Lampwick, he took me to the Inn of the Red Lobster.

GEPPETTO: You ain't gonna believe your old papa, but I met these two people, and one of them looked a lot like a fox . . .

PINOCCHIO: The Fox and the Cat! They were there, too.

GEPPETTO: And they said, "Pinocchio? Pinocchio's gone away in a boat, across the sea."

PINOCCHIO: To Paradise Island, Papa. To the Island of Boys.

GEPPETTO: So I got *me* a boat, but this great big whale came and opened its mouth and swallowed your Papa up — boat and all!

PINOCCHIO: To the Island of *Real* Boys, Papa. But they all turned into . . . into . . .

(Pinocchio turns away from Geppetto and the old man sees a donkey's tail growing from behind Pinocchio.)

GEPPETTO: Pinocchio! You got a tail! A donkey tail!

PINOCCHIO: *(Crying; hugging Geppetto.)* Oh, Papa!

GEPPETTO: *(Holding him close; patting his back.)* Oh, Pinocchio — that's all right . . . that's all right . . . at least now we are together. We can be together . . . before . . . we die . . .

PINOCCHIO: *(Lifting his head up.)* Die?! What do you mean, Papa? We gotta get out of here!

GEPPETTO: *(Standing and walking away, frustrated.)* We *can't* get out of here, Pinocchio; don't you know? It's hopeless! It's hopeless!

PINOCCHIO: But I can't let you die here, Papa!

GEPPETTO: Oh, warm our hands by the fire.

PINOCCHIO: *(His chin cupped in his hands, staring at the tiny fire on the floor before him.)* Oh, if only . . . if only there were . . . (A pause. An idea.) Papa! Papa — the fire!

GEPPETTO: *(Flatly, not paying attention.)* That's right, the fire.
(Pinocchio quickly grabs more wood and sets it on the fire.)

GEPPETTO: Pinocchio! Hey, Pinocchio — whadda you doing?

PINOCCHIO: Build up the fire, Papa! We'll make lots of smoke, and maybe the whale will sneeze!

GEPPETTO: *Sneeze?!* You crazy!

(*Pinocchio pays no attention; he keeps breaking wood and tossing it on the pile.*)

GEPPETTO: It *might work* . . .

PINOCCHIO: Help me, Papa!

GEPPETTO: Yes! Yes, we need more wood, don't we? *(Joining in, excited.)* Here . . . the stool, Pinocchio; put that on, we don't need it.

PINOCCHIO: And the fishing pole!

GEPPETTO: Look, Pinocchio! Smoke! It's working!

PINOCCHIO: Fan the fire, Papa!

(*Geppetto uses his shawl to fan the fire. A great cloud of smoke rises and begins to fill the belly of the whale. The walls of the whale's belly begin to shudder and we hear the distant, increasing sound of a sneeze coming on.*)

GEPPETTO: Listen!

(*Pinocchio and Geppetto cock their heads and listen intently.*)

PINOCCHIO: Papa! It's going to sneeze! Papa — the whale is going to sneeze us out!

GEPPETTO: *(Clutching Pinocchio close to him.)* Hold on to me, Pinocchio! Hold on! I can't swim! Hold on!

PINOCCHIO: Look out, Papa! Hold on tight!

(*The sound has increased and mounted to one, gigantic sneeze. The raft quickly retreats upstage as lights simultaneously black out. Music swells and on the scrim we see flying patterns of swirling water and debris. The sound of violently rushing water and the indistinct cries of Pinocchio and Geppetto calling each other's names.*)

the Portrait the Wind the Chair
Y York

In this wonderfully imaginative play, little Lucy and her older sister, Terroba, find themselves stranded in their "gramma's" old house during the worst windstorm of the century. As the storm intensifies, nothing remains the same: an old chair develops a mind of its own. Gramma pops out of her portrait, and Lucy grows in her understanding of fear and the power of love.

Two Females

In the two scenes that follow, which open the play, Lucy and her sister, Terroba, begin their night in Gramma's old house.

+ + +

This living room/dining room of a house, a little run-down, simply furnished, and with a lot of houseplants. There is a life-size portrait of a teenage girl with short, curled hair, white socks, saddle oxfords, flare skirt, sweater, and pearls (circa 1950). It is a comfortable room. The sound of a ferocious wind storm. Wind. Lucy, carrying her book bag and the mail, opens the door, sticks in her head, shouts.

LUCY: Terroba! *(Pause.)* Hey! *(Pause.)*
(Lucy comes in cautiously, carefully locks the doors behind her. She stands there a moment, not knowing what to do. Then she uses her coat as a barrier between herself and the portrait as she goes to the kitchen.)
LUCY: Don't look at me like that. I don't even see you up there. And your stupid chair isn't going to get me either. *(She punches the chair.)* So there!

(Exits to kitchen. Terroba, fourteen, enters, she looks exactly like the girl in the portrait. She is angry with herself.)

TERROBA: Stupid, stupid, stupid. *(She hangs up her coat, then self-mocking.)* "Hey Emily, wanna come over and do homework like the old days." Stupid, stupid, stupid.

(Unseen, Lucy stands in the kitchen doorway, still with letters, book bag, and also a broom.)

LUCY: Who you talking to?

(Terroba screams.)

LUCY: *(Screams.)* Don't scare me! Don't scare me!

TERROBA: Scare *you? (Beat.)* What are you doing here?! You have tutoring!

LUCY: No tutoring. Because of the storm.

(Terroba starts upstairs.)

TERROBA: *(With finality.)* I've got homework.

(Lucy remains where she is with coat on, throws newspaper and mail on the floor. Terroba stops.)

TERROBA: What? What now?

LUCY: You know what.

TERROBA: *(Sighs.)* You have to get over this.

LUCY: Well, I'm not over it *yet.* OK?!

(Terroba opens closet.)

TERROBA: *(Overloud for Lucy's benefit.)* What have we here? Coats coats and more coats. And overshoes and boots. And coat hangers. All monsters have taken up residence elsewhere.

(Terroba starts to close closet.)

LUCY: Not so fast.

(Lucy pokes in closet with broom. She jumps back frightened.)

LUCY: Oh!

TERROBA: What?

LUCY: *(Realizing.)* Oh, it's just a jacket. OK.

TERROBA: Give me your coat.

(Terroba tries to take Lucy's coat.)

LUCY: Don't touch me.

TERROBA: I was just going to hang it up.

LUCY: Here.

(Lucy tosses the coat on floor. Terroba hangs it up.)

TERROBA: You are so messy. Put that stuff *(Letters.)* on the table.

LUCY: I don't know why I have to bring in the letters every day.

TERROBA: Because it's your job.

LUCY: I'm not allowed to read them, why should I have to bring them in?

TERROBA: *(For the tenth time.)* You bring them in so the house looks occupied. If you leave letters in the box, we're sitting ducks.

LUCY: We're sitting ducks just from the letters?

TERROBA: Letters in the box make you a target.

LUCY: Then the mailman shouldn't leave them!

TERROBA: It's his job to leave them. It's your job to bring them in so the house looks occupied. I'm going upstairs.

LUCY: *(Worried.)* No. Poke under the chair first.

(Lucy holds out the broom. Terroba takes it and pokes under the chair.)

TERROBA: Poke, poke, poke. OK?

LUCY: You'll thank me when there's something under there someday.

TERROBA: There's nothing under anything, Lucy. Should I poke under the sofa?

LUCY: Why?

TERROBA: In case there's something under it!

LUCY: Don't be ridiculous. Nothing's under the *sofa.*

(Lucy kicks the chair.)

TERROBA: Lucy!

LUCY: Who cares! It's a crummy old chair. Send it to the dump.

TERROBA: Gramma liked it.

(Terroba sits and sinks down into the chair.)

LUCY: *(To chair.)* Oh no. Let her go! You let her go!

TERROBA: What?!

LUCY: Give me your hand! I'll pull you out!

TERROBA: I can get out. Lucy, calm down.

LUCY: Oh. I thought it was pulling you down.

TERROBA: No. It's not pulling, it's fine. *(Bounces.)* A little lumpy maybe, but fine.

LUCY: It's a *lot* lumpy. How could Gramma even stand to sit in it?

TERROBA: Maybe the lumps fit her behind.

LUCY: Well they don't fit mine.

TERROBA: *(To chair.)* You sure are a lumpy chair.

LUCY: *(Mad.)* Oh great, now *you're* talkin' to the chair! Are you gonna turn loopy like Gramma before she died? "Looks like it's just you and me; these grandchildren are too busy for us. Don't mind me, Lucy, me and my old chair are having a little chat."

TERROBA: Probably because *you* wouldn't talk to her.

LUCY: Stop blaming me!

TERROBA: Nobody's *blaming* anybody. *(Beat, examining chair.)* This chair is a wreck. Maybe we could get it reupholstered or something.

LUCY: I hate it.

TERROBA: We'll add it to the list of stuff to hate around here. *(As she starts upstairs.)* Don't make a mess. Mom's gotta talk to the chairman today.

LUCY: She's gonna be in a bad mood.

TERROBA: That's why don't make a mess.

LUCY: *(To keep Terroba in the room.)* Yeah, she hates the chairman.

TERROBA: *(Returning.)* She doesn't *hate* him. Where do you come up with these things?

LUCY: She does. Because of the suit thing — the suit thing.

TERROBA: What? . . . Suit affliction?

LUCY: Yeah; he's got *suit affliction*. A fatal case.

TERROBA: Lucy — Suit affliction is a *joke* — when nobody respects you, you put on a suit to get some respect.

LUCY: I don't hear a joke in that.

TERROBA: You're too little.

LUCY: You hate the chairman, too. He makes you so nervous you can't study.

TERROBA: I don't hate him; he doesn't *have* to give money for getting As.

LUCY: Would he give me a hundred dollars for college if I get an A?

TERROBA: *(Exasperated.)* It's a program. Any kid gets an A, gets a hundred dollars. But the way you study, his hundred dollars is pretty safe. *(Heading upstairs.)* No mess, Lucy, no kidding.

LUCY: Let me come be in your room.

TERROBA: No.

LUCY: I'll be silent. Not a word. Zip.

TERROBA: That's what you said last time.

✦　✦　✦

Terroba exits upstairs, leaving the broom behind. Lucy gets an idea. She takes the broom for protectoin, makes threatening gestures to the chair and portrait as she goes. Lucy drags dining chairs away from the table, takes the afghan from the back of the sofa, tosses it on the chairs to make a cave. Goes to the closet with her broom, gingerly opens it, pokes inside, takes out Mom's suit jacket and ties up the chair with it. All of her unspoken activities are punctuated by her own soundtrack [humming].

LUCY: *(To chair, while tying it up.)* You won't stay in our house if I have anything to say about it. You'll go right in the soonest garbage truck. There! That should hold you forever.

(She pulls an old suitcase from the closet, opens it, takes a half slip from inside and puts it on her head, wearing the slip like its hair; takes out alligator shoes, growls, places them strategically. Walks in a queenly fashion.)

LUCY: The Queen of the Amazon proclaims tomorrow a no-school day for all public school children in America.

(Terroba enters with her book.)

TERROBA: Do you want something to eat — what's on the chair?

LUCY: That is not a chair; that is a prisoner of war. Caught trying to assassinate her highness.

(Terroba unties the chair and hangs up the jacket.)

TERROBA: You're gonna ruin Mom's good jacket.

LUCY: She never wears it.

TERROBA: You're still not allowed to play with it.

LUCY: The Queen of the Amazon may play with anything she likes.

TERROBA: The Queen of the Amazon wears a slip on her head?

LUCY: This is my long flowing hair. *(Big voice.)* You must obey my every commandment.

TERROBA: Like: thou shalt not slay thy bossy little sister?

LUCY: *(Big voice.)* Don't enrage the Queen, or you wilt be sorry.

TERROBA: Is this the mess I told you not to make! *(Suspicious.)* Where did you get Gramma's alligator shoes?

LUCY: Not shoes. Dangerous man-eating reptiles along the river bank.

TERROBA: Is that Gramma Minnie's slip?

LUCY: Hair!

TERROBA: Is it Gramma's?

LUCY: It was in her suitcase.

TERROBA: You're not supposed to be in Gramma's stuff.

LUCY: Why? She doesn't need it.

TERROBA: Chill, Lucy. Just chill.

LUCY: I can play with it if I want.

TERROBA: Mom won't like it.

LUCY: Well, who's going to tell her, snitch face?

(Terroba crosses and looks in suitcase as Lucy gets large books from the book case which she spreads along the floor in a long path. She steps from book to book. They talk over the action.)

LUCY: *(Lying.)* Besides, Gramma said I could have anything I want. Anything in her suitcase. She said so.

TERROBA: *(Suspicious.)* When did you two have this conversation?

LUCY: *Before she died.* When do you think? Yesterday?

TERROBA: You never even went in her room. The whole time she was sick.

LUCY: I'm little; I don't have to talk to sick people.

TERROBA: It was fun to talk to her.

LUCY: It wasn't fun. It was scary.

TERROBA: You weren't too scared when she took you to the lake. You weren't too scared when she took you to the movies.

LUCY: I was too scared. The whole time.

TERROBA: You weren't. Not 'til she got sick. As soon as Gramma couldn't take you places — Zip! — you don't go in her room. I don't know why she wanted you to have anything.

LUCY: She didn't give me anything.

TERROBA: She gave you this house.

LUCY: Mom still has to pay the mortgage, and besides she didn't give it to *me*; she hated me.

TERROBA: If she hated you then why did she want you to have the ring with the beautiful blue stone?

LUCY: Because the ring with the beautiful blue stone doesn't exist, that's why. It's easy to give somebody something that doesn't exist.

TERROBA: *(To herself.)* She gave me the tiny little diamond.

LUCY: There's no tiny little diamond, either. It was fever dreams.

TERROBA: I know! *(Beat.)* She was pretty sick there at the end.

LUCY: Sick and mean.

TERROBA: What did Gramma ever do to you.

LUCY: She *died*, she died to me.

TERROBA: She couldn't help it. You are a crumb.

LUCY: I'm not — listen, if she wanted me to have a ring with a beautiful blue stone, she for sure wanted me to have her *slip*.

TERROBA: You better not hurt Mom's law books.

LUCY: I must step carefully from rock to rock so I don't get eaten. *(Referring to shoes.)* The River Amazon is full of alligators.

TERROBA: Not really. It's too full of pollution now.

LUCY: Well, *my* River Amazon is full of alligators!

TERROBA: *(Thoughtful, at suitcase.)* Maybe Gramma always wanted a tiny little diamond, or something. Hey! Maybe there's a secret hidden compartment. For rings.

(Lucy goes to the suitcase. They poke around; find pearls, scarves.)

LUCY: It's just an old cardboard suitcase. There's no secret compartment.

TERROBA: She let me wear these pearls once.

LUCY: Big deal.

TERROBA: *(At portrait.)* No, they're very old. She's got them on in her picture. That's how old.

LUCY: How come you got to wear them?

TERROBA: It was for Halloween. I was an oyster.

LUCY: Oh, yeah, *weird!*

TERROBA: No, it was very clever. It was Gramma's idea.

LUCY: *(Mad.)* Yeah, she's the one talked me into being a mushroom.

(Lucy takes a cushion from the sofa and puts it on her head. It makes her look remarkably like a toadstool.)

TERROBA: I thought that was your own idea.

LUCY: Nope. *(Points to portrait.)* Hers. She guaranteed nobody else would be one. *(Sarcastic.)* She was right!

TERROBA: Let's put this stuff away. You've turned the living room into a dump.

LUCY: No I haven't; dumps are outside. Let's play with it before we put it away.

TERROBA: The house has to be nice for when Mom gets home.

LUCY: Come on, just for a little while. Then I'll help you straighten up. Come on.

(Lucy tempts Terroba with a second slip.)

TERROBA: *(Checks clock.)* Oh, all right, but just for a little while. *(Terroba puts slip on head. Lucy is excited that she's tricked Terroba into playing.)*

LUCY: I'll be in my queen cage. You must come and pay my homage.

TERROBA: Pay your homage?

LUCY: Yeah, come in to my cave and pay it. You can pay it with your fabulous silken scarves.

TERROBA: That's not what pay homage means.

LUCY: Who cares?

TERROBA: Well, not you, if your vocabulary score is evidence.

LUCY: Be careful of the alligators. Step only on the rocks.

TERROBA: I, Terroba, Queen of the lesser Amazon, come to the cave of Lucy —

(Lucy threatens Terroba with the alligator shoes; she growls.)

TERROBA: Are you a Queen or alligators?

(Lucy growls.)

TERROBA: Alligators are silent, Lucy.

LUCY: Don't call me Lucy. Lucy is too stupid for a queen.

TERROBA: Not as stupid as Terrrora. I told Mom and Dad to call you Lucy or don't bring you home from the hospital.

LUCY: It's stupid.

TERROBA: It was the best I could do on short notice. Mom and Dad were going to call you End-all-war.

LUCY: Call me something better.

TERROBA: I, Terroba, Queen of the lesser Amazon, come to the cave of *Lucinderoba. (Lucy squeals with delight and runs to cave.)* Queen of the major Amazon, to pay homage and give her my fabulous silken scarves.

LUCY: Hum something.

(Terroba hums as Lucy marches along the rocks in grand fashion.)

LUCY: I, Lucinderoba, Queen of the Amazon, do take your fabulous homage.

(These is a terrible crash. The girls scream and grab each other.)

LUCY: *(Gaining control of herself.)* Let me go.

TERROBA: You hugged me first.

(Terroba crosses to the door.)

LUCY: *(Worried.)* Where are you *going?*

TERROBA: I want to see what that was.

(They cross to the front door. Open it. It's monstrous windy, loud. They see that a tree has fallen. They are impressed and scared. Close door.)

LUCY: Man! That was *close!*

TERROBA: *(To cover fear.)* It's not so close.

LUCY: It almost fell on the house!

TERROBA: It wouldn't have fallen on the house even if it fell the other way.

LUCY: Right into the living room!

The Rememberer
Steven Dietz

Set in 1911, *The Rememberer* is based on the memoirs of Joyce Simmons Cheeka, a young Native American girl who was forcibly taken from her home and put in a government training school. Told in flashbacks between the young Joyce and an older Joyce, the cruelty of a dark chapter in American history unfolds, revealing the strong bonds that can tie a family together despite seemingly insurmountable odds. In the end, Joyce emerges to carry on the family tradition as the rememberer.

Four Females

Here, Joyce and three other girls in the government training school share a practical joke out of the watchful eye of the matron in charge.

+ + +

A trumpet plays "Reveille." Morning. Lights reveal the washroom, again — as Joyce enters in line behind the three other girls. They bring their tin boxes with them, as before. Nurse Warner, as before, walks down the line and gives them their tooth powder. They begin to brush their teeth, identically, as before. Nurse Warner leaves. The girls are alone. They immediately turn and start talking to each other — now brushing any way they want to.

GIRL TWO: You were laughing, I saw you!
JOYCE: You were laughing louder!
YOUNG GIRL: Laughing at what?
GIRL TWO: At the fish oil!

(Joyce and Girl Two laugh as — Girl One quiets them, quickly.)

GIRL ONE: *(An urgent whisper.)* Quiet. She's here —

(The girls straighten up and brush their teeth very formally, as — Miss Brennan looks in on them.)

MISS BRENNAN: No Indian words, girls. You know better.

(Miss Brennan checks her hair in their mirror, quickly. She also gives the perfume on her wrist a quick sniff. She smiles.)

MISS BRENNAN: I'll see you in class.

(Miss Brennan goes, the girls relax.)

GIRL ONE: You did not!

GIRL TWO: Yes, I did!

YOUNG GIRL: What? Did what?

GIRL ONE: Who saw you?

GIRL TWO: Joyce saw me.

YOUNG GIRL: What? Saw what?

GIRL TWO: Tell her.

JOYCE: Yeah. I saw her.

GIRL ONE: Really?

JOYCE: Yeah.

YOUNG GIRL: What? Saw her do what?

GIRL TWO: Tell her, Joyce.

JOYCE: She found a bottle of Miss Brennan's perfume.

GIRL ONE: So?

JOYCE: And she dumped out the perfume and filled it with fish oil.

YOUNG GIRL: Really?

GIRL ONE: *(To Girl Two.)* Did she get mad?

JOYCE: She hasn't noticed!

(The girls laugh even louder. They finish brushing their teeth and hair during the following.)

GIRL ONE: Darin Longfeather showed me the scars on his back.

(The girls laugh a bit.)

JOYCE: What scars?

GIRL ONE: It's not funny. The scars from his other school. Where they whipped him with a belt.

(The girls are more serious, now.)

JOYCE: Why'd they do that?

GIRL ONE: I don't know. But, they did. I *saw.* That's why he ran away.

JOYCE: They caught him and sent him here.

GIRL TWO: I bet he runs away again.

GIRL ONE: The Sheriff'll kill him if he does. Darin said so.

JOYCE: Dr. Buchanan wouldn't let them hurt him.

GIRL TWO: They can do whatever they want, Joyce. It doesn't matter what the teachers say.

GIRL ONE: Darin said there's no way he'll get caught.

JOYCE: What do you mean?

GIRL ONE: He says he knows a trail. A secret trail that will get him home.

(A bell rings. The girls file out in a line.)

Still Life with Iris
Steven Dietz

In this multifaceted and highly symbolic play, Iris lives in the mysterious land of Nocturno, where people create their own worlds as they sleep. Each person has a particular job: there is the Thunder Bottler, the Leaf Monitor, and the Rain Maker. All are assigned to find the perfect example of their work, which they must send to their rulers, Grotto and Gretta Good, who live on the Island of Great Goods. Iris is sent as the "perfect" daughter, but she must leave her coat behind, for it holds all the memories of Nocturno within its folds. When Iris keeps one of the buttons, the memories of family haunt her, and thus begins her journey of self-discovery.

One Male and Three Females (and one nonspeaking part)

In the first scene below, Iris comes before Grotto and Gretta Good, the rulers of the Island of Great Goods, looking for one of her shoes, which is missing. One of Good's servants, Mister Otherguy, attend them. In the second scene, Iris encounters Annabel Lee, a young woman of the sea, who has been held captive for many years.

✦ ✦ ✦

The door flies open quickly, revealing Iris. She now wears an overlayer of clothing that is similar to the Great Goods — elegantly eccentric, very different than her Nocturno attire. She wears one very shiny shoe. The Goods gesture for her to take a step into the room. She does so. She stands stiffly, with a pleasant, forced smile on her face. The clock chimes, once. For a moment, they all just stand and nod at each other. Finally, Iris turns to Grotto Good and speaks in as friendly a way as possible.

IRIS: Hello. I'm Iris. What an odd place this is.
(Grotto nods at her for a moment, then turns quickly to Otherguy.)
GROTTO GOOD: My good, *she said something to me.*
(Otherguy gestures for Grotto to respond. Grotto looks at Iris, looks at Gretta, looks back at Iris . . . then finally speaks, smilingly, definitively.)
GROTTO GOOD: You are a girl.
IRIS: Yes.
GROTTO GOOD: *(Smiling throughout.)* And now you are here.
IRIS: Yes, I am.
GROTTO GOOD: And I am speaking to you.
IRIS: Yes, you are.
GROTTO GOOD: *(Still smiling.)* And now I am finished. *(Turns to his wife.)* Gretta?
GRETTA GOOD: *(Walks toward Iris, calmly.)* You must forgive my husband. He's never spoken to a little girl before. You are the first one to ever arrive on Great Island.
IRIS: I see.
GRETTA GOOD: But, you are welcome here, Iris. More than welcome, you are *treasured.*
GROTTO GOOD: You will now be the greatest of our goods.
IRIS: Umm . . . thank you . . .
GRETTA GOOD: And?
IRIS: And where's my other shoe?
GROTTO GOOD: Oh, my.
GRETTA GOOD: You are wearing the finest shoe under the sky. Have you *looked* at it?
IRIS: Yes, I have, and it's beautiful — maybe the most beautiful shoe I've ever seen. But, still, one of them is missing and

the one I'm wearing really hurts my foot. Is there another pair I could wear?

GROTTO GOOD: Oh, my.

IRIS: They don't have to be as nice as these —

GROTTO GOOD: Oh, my.

IRIS: Just a little more comfortable, so I —

GRETTA GOOD: Iris.

IRIS: Yes, Mother Good?

GRETTA GOOD: There are no other shoes for you. We have only what's BEST on this island and to ensure the value and importance of each item, *we have only one of everything. (To Otherguy.)* Bring her something to drink. *(Otherguy nods and brings a goblet, as well as a small, sealed glass container, on a tray to Iris.)*

IRIS: One of everything — what do you mean?

GROTTO GOOD: Look around, Iris! Everything here is unrivaled in its goodness. Like, for example, our BOOK. Or this — our DRAPE. Or our CHAIR.

IRIS: You have only one chair?

GROTTO GOOD: Isn't it a beauty? *(He brings it to her and insists she sit in it during the following.)*

GRETTA GOOD: So, you see, Iris, that is why you have only one shoe.

IRIS: What happened to its mate?

GROTTO GOOD: It is now in the Tunnel of the Unwanted.

GRETTA GOOD: *(Sees that Iris's drink is ready.)* Oh, here we are. Thirsty?

IRIS: Very.

(Otherguy offers Iris the goblet. She takes it and looks in it — it is empty. Otherguy opens the sealed glass container. He tips it over and pours its contents into the goblet: one long, slow, perfect drop of water. The Goods nod approvingly, as Iris looks into the goblet.)

IRIS: What is this?

GROTTO GOOD: It's a perfect raindrop.

IRIS: This is all the water you have?

GRETTA GOOD: It's all we need. For, at daybreak, another perfect drop will arrive. There's a land near here where they work all night to see to our pleasure each day.

GROTTO GOOD: So, drink up!

(Iris looks at them, looks at the goblet, then drinks. She, of course, barely tastes it. As she swallows, the Goods sigh, audibly, blissfully.)

GRETTA GOOD: Perfect, isn't it?

IRIS: I guess.

GRETTA GOOD: Now, Iris, we've heard you have a gift for finding things. Is that true?

IRIS: I don't know. Maybe. I don't remember finding *anything*.

GROTTO GOOD: You'll help us find PERFECT THINGS for the Island, I'm sure. Now, we've prepared the best of the best for you —

IRIS: What exactly do you *do* here?

GRETTA GOOD: We enjoy our goods in the greatest of ways.

IRIS: Don't you work?

GROTTO GOOD: Certainly not.

GRETTA GOOD: But we are ever on the lookout for flaws. We mustn't let anything that is not the BEST invade Great Island. *(Gretta sees the pouch that Iris wears.)* Like *this* for example. What is the meaning of this old pouch?

GROTTO GOOD: And what's inside?

IRIS: A button. It belongs to a little girl I'm looking for.

GROTTO GOOD: There are no other girls, Iris. You're the only one here.

GRETTA GOOD: Mister Otherguy, show Iris her toy box.

(Otherguy raises the lid of the toy box, as Iris continues to stare at Grotto.)

IRIS: There's no one else to play with?

GRETTA GOOD: We're still searching for a little boy.

GROTTO GOOD: One who's perfect — like you.

IRIS: You brought me here because you think I'm perfect?

GROTTO GOOD: Of course we did.

IRIS: I'm not perfect.

GRETTA GOOD: *(After a quick look at Grotto.) Really?*

IRIS: Not perfect at all.

GROTTO GOOD: Very well. Tell us something you've done that *wasn't perfect.* Some day when you did a bad thing. Something from your *past*, Iris.

(The Goods look at her.)

GROTTO GOOD: Well?

(Silence. Iris thinks.)

IRIS: I can't think of anything.

GROTTO GOOD: You see!

IRIS: But, I know I'm not —

(The Goods leave happily, in a flourish, saying —)

GROTTO GOOD: Enjoy your toys, Iris!

GRETTA GOOD: And if you find anything that is not the BEST of its kind —

GROTTO GOOD: We'll discard and replace it immediately!

GRETTA GOOD: A great good pleasure to meet you!

GROTTO GOOD: A great good pleasure, indeed!

(Music, as lights pull down to isolate Iris near the toy box. The face of the clock remains lit, as well. Mister Otherguy lifts something out of the toy box: a doll encased in glass. On the side of the glass is a small lock. The doll is dressed identically to Iris. Otherguy holds the doll out to Iris. Iris looks at him . . . then takes it from him. She looks at the doll, then tries to open the lock to take the doll from the case — but it won't open.)

IRIS: It's locked. How can I play with her if she's locked inside?

(Mister Otherguy simply shrugs and exits.)

✦   ✦   ✦

Annabel Lee, a young woman of the sea, appears. She wears a tattered gown of dark blues and greens and the boots and belt of a pirate. Her belt holds a small telescope. Her hair is entwined with seaweed. And, most prominently, she has a long chain (or rope) attached to her wrist, or ankle, with a large padlock, which leads far out into the sea, offstage. Iris stares at her, amazed.

ANNABEL LEE: *(As she enters.)* In a kingdom by the sea. Have you never seen an Annabel Lee?

IRIS: Never. How did you —

ANNABEL LEE: For years I've been locked away — held against my will — but now you, Iris, you've set me free.

IRIS: How?

ANNABEL LEE: By loosing these chains that bind me to the sea.

IRIS: But how did you get here?

ANNABEL LEE: Through your wishing, I assume. What else could it be?

IRIS: I did wish for someone to play with. And I wished for someone to help me get across this water.

ANNABEL LEE: And I wished I would find my ship.

IRIS: You have a ship?

ANNABEL LEE: *(Looking through her telescope.)* It's what I'm searching for, and my ship is searching for me.

IRIS: How do you know?

ANNABEL LEE: I listen at night, locked away, in my kingdom by the sea.

And as the waves crash and fall —

I can hear in the squall —

My ship's voice calling to me —

IRIS: What does it say?

ANNABEL LEE: For the moon never beams without bringing me dreams
Of the beautiful Annabel Lee;
And the stars never rise, but I see the bright eyes
Of my captain, Annabel Lee.

IRIS: *(Smiles.)* Your ship really calls out to you?

ANNABEL LEE: I'm so close to finding it, Iris. It's just out of reach.

IRIS: I see a picture like that, sometimes. A picture of a room. But I don't know where it is.

ANNABEL LEE: What have you been using to navigate with? Have you been using the stars?

IRIS: There's more than *one?*

ANNABEL LEE: Of course there are. Look.
(She hands Iris the telescope, and Iris looks through it at a sky full of stars.)

IRIS: Oh, my. From the palace of the Great Goods, you can only see *one* star.

ANNABEL LEE: Why is that?

IRIS: It's the best one. They chose it.

ANNABEL LEE: There's no best in stars. They're like the waves upon the sea. A multitude of many; far as the eye can see. *(Shakes the chain with her arm.)* Now, if you'll free me from this, I'll find my ship and together we'll sail away.
(Iris goes to her and tries to pry the lock from Annabel Lee's arm.)

IRIS: It's locked shut. Maybe we could cut the chain.

ANNABEL LEE: It's too strong — I've tried.

IRIS: *(Looks closely at the lock.)* Then we have to pick the lock. We need something long and narrow and flat. *(Iris looks around, but sees nothing that will work.)*

ANNABEL LEE: Maybe something in your pouch?

IRIS: *(Showing her.)* All I have is this button. *(Still looking.)* There must be *something* we can use.

ANNABEL LEE: *(Looking up to the sky.)* I think I know what it is.

IRIS: You do?

(Annabel Lee nods.)

IRIS: What is it?

(Annabel Lee sits, leaning against the shell, looking up at the stars.)

ANNABEL LEE: The same thing that brought me here to you.

IRIS: But that was me — wishing.

ANNABEL LEE: Exactly. *(Gestures for Iris to join her.)* C'mon Iris. Your wishes will be our vessel. And the stars will be our map. And with courage and faith as our captain and mate, the ship I've lost and room you seek may fall into our laps. *(Annabel Lee begins to hum "Twinkle Twinkle Little Star," softly and beautifully. After a moment, Iris sits next to her and joins her. They whistle/hum the song together, happily.)*

There's a Boy in the Girls' Bathroom
Louis Sachar

Based on his novel of the same name, Louis Sachar's play tells the tale of Bradley Chalkers, a compulsive liar and all around class misfit who seems headed for a year of disaster. But, with the help of Carla, the school counselor, and Jeff, a new boy who befriends him despite peer pressure, Bradley learns to manage his lying and, most of all, his fears.

Two Males and Three Females

In the first scene, Bradley encounters Jeff, the boy who will eventually help him overcome his troubles. In the scene that follows, Bradley talks with Carla, his counselor.

✦ ✦ ✦

This scene begins in the hallway at school, moves to the girls' bathroom, then back through the hall to the counselor's office. The hallway is suggested by the backs of the three movable sets, staggered on stage. As Jeff moves from one location to the other, that set revolves to greet him.

Jeff enters hallway, lost. He starts one direction, then turns around and starts to go back the way he came. He is about to exit, then suddenly stops as if he sees something that has scared him. He quickly backs away toward center stage. What Jeff had seen was Bradley who now enters.

BRADLEY: Jeff!
JEFF: *(Jeff looks around for a teacher or someone to save him. He's scared of Bradley but tries to sound brave.)* Just leave

me alone, Bradley. I don't have any more money and even if I did I wouldn't give it to you.

BRADLEY: Where you goin'?

JEFF: I'm trying to find the counselor's office. And I'm already late.

BRADLEY: Ooh, she's going to be mad. She's real mean. And ugly.

JEFF: Have you already seen her?

BRADLEY: Me? Why would I have to see a counselor? I didn't do anything wrong!

JEFF: Uh, I just thought Mrs. Ebbel — Well I have to see her. She's supposed to help me "adjust to my new environment." *(Short laugh.)*

BRADLEY: That's stupid.

(Jeff starts to leave.)

BRADLEY: Jeff.

(Jeff stops.)

BRADLEY: I'll give you a dollar, if you'll be my friend.

(Jeff is too stunned to answer. Bradley reaches in his pocket and holds out a dollar. Jeff stares at it a moment then reaches out and takes it.)

JEFF: *(Looks at the dollar in his hand.)* If you want, I can help you with your homework sometime. I know I'm new here, but I'm pretty smart, and we learned the same stuff at my old school. *(He shrugs modestly.)*

BRADLEY: *(Looking at Jeff like he was crazy.)* I don't need any help. I'm the smartest kid in class. Ask anyone. *(Exits.)*

(Jeff puts the dollar in pocket. Sighs and rubs his face. Mrs. Ebbel enters carrying a stack of papers.)

JEFF: *(Frantic, yet polite.)* Excuse me, Mrs. Ebbel. Can you tell me where the counselor's office is, please.

MRS. EBBEL: The counselor's office . . . Let's see. Go down this hall to the end. Turn right, and it's the third door on your left.

JEFF: Thank you very much. *(He starts to go as he talks to himself.)* Right, third door.

MRS. EBBEL: No wait. That's not right. She's in the new office in the other wing. Turn around and go back the way you came, go right, then turn left at the end of the hall and it's the door immediately to your right.

JEFF: Thank you.

(Mrs. Ebbel exits. Jeff turns around and moves across the stage talking to himself.)

JEFF: Turn right. Third door on left. *(Enters girls' bathroom.)* I'm sorry I'm late.

(Colleen is buttoning her pants as she steps out of a stall.)

COLLEEN: What are you doing in here?

JEFF: *(It hasn't registered yet where he is.)* Huh?

COLLEEN: Get out of here! This is the girls' bathroom!

(Jeff stands frozen a moment then exits, running.)

COLLEEN: *(After Jeff has already left.)* THERE'S A BOY IN THE GIRLS' BATHROOM! *(She shouts it one or two more times as the set revolves away, taking her with it. Jeff moves through the hall and backs into the counselor's office. The office is a mess, cluttered with boxes and papers. The walls are blank bulletin boards. There is a round table with two chairs. There is also a stool. Carla is putting something up on bulletin board but stops to greet Jeff who has his back to her.)*

CARLA: You must be Jeff.

(Startled, Jeff turns to face her.)

CARLA: I'm Carla Davis.

(She holds out her hand. Jeff numbly shakes it.)

CARLA: Come in.

(Carla indicates for Jeff to have a seat and they both sit down around the round table.)

CARLA: You'll have to excuse the mess. I'm still getting moved in.

(Jeff stares blankly at her.)

CARLA: So how do you like Red Hill School so far?

(Jeff is numb and dumb.)

CARLA: I imagine it must seem a little scary. I think it's scary. It seems so big! Anytime I try to go anywhere, I get lost.

(Jeff smiles weakly — if she only knew.)

CARLA: It's hard for me because I'm new here. I don't know anybody. Nobody knows me. The other teachers all look at me strangely. I think some of them don't understand what a counselor does. It's hard for me to make friends with them. They already have their own friends.

(Jeff nods along.)

CARLA: Maybe you can help me?

JEFF: Me? How can *I* help *you*. You're supposed to help me.

CARLA: Maybe we can help each other. What do you think about that?

(Jeff smiles and shrugs.)

CARLA: We're the two new kids at school. We can share our experiences and learn from each other.

JEFF: OK, Miss Davis.

CARLA: Jeff, if we're going to be friends, I want you to call me Carla, not Miss Davis.

(Jeff laughs.)

CARLA: Do you think Carla is a funny name?

JEFF: Oh, no! I just never called a teacher by her first name, that's all.

CARLA: But we're friends. Friends don't call each other Miss Davis and Mr. Fishkin, do they?

JEFF: *(Laughs again.)* The kids in my class all call me Fishface.

CARLA: Have you made any friends?

JEFF: One. But I don't like him.

CARLA: How can be be your friend if you don't like him?

JEFF: Nobody likes him. At first I felt sorry for him because nobody even wants to sit near him. Mrs. Ebbel said so.

CARLA: It must have hurt his feelings.

JEFF: No, he just smiled.

CARLA: He may have been smiling on the outside, but do you think he really was smiling on the inside?

JEFF: I don't know. I guess not. I guess that's why I tried to be friends with him. I told him I didn't mind sitting by him. But then he said, "Give me a dollar or I'll spit on you!"

CARLA: What'd you do?

JEFF: *(Obviously, as if he had no choice.)* I gave him a dollar. I didn't want to get spit on. But then, today, he said, "I'll give you a dollar if you'll be my friend."

CARLA: What'd you do?

JEFF: *(Obviously.)* I took it. *(Pause.)* So does that mean I have to be his friend, even though I just broke even?

CARLA: What do you think friendship is?

JEFF: I don't know. I mean I know what it is, but I can't explain it.

CARLA: Is it something you can buy or sell? Can you go to the store and get a quart of milk, a dozen eggs, and a friend?

JEFF: *(Laughing.)* No. So does that mean I don't have to be his friend? I don't even know if Bradley wants to be friends.

CARLA: I think you'll find that if you're nice to Bradley, he'll be nice to you. It's just like with the dollar. You always break even.

✦ ✦ ✦

CARLA: Bradley Chalkers . . . *(She reads something in the file that makes her laugh.)*

BRADLEY: *(Entering.)* I'm here, whadda ya' want?

CARLA: *(Stands and smiles warmly at him.)* Hello, Bradley. I'm Carla Davis. It's a pleasure to see you today. *(She holds out her hand for him to shake.)* I've been looking forward to meeting you.

(Bradley just stares at her.)

CARLA: Aren't you going to shake my hand?

BRADLEY: Nah, you're too ugly.

(He walks past her and sits down at the round table. Carla sits across from him.)

CARLA: I appreciate your coming to see me.

BRADLEY: I had to come. Mrs. Ebbel made me.

CARLA: For whatever reason, I'm glad you came.

BRADLEY: I meant to go to the library. I came here by accident.

CARLA: Oh, I don't believe in accidents.

BRADLEY: *(Looks at her funny.)* What about when you spill your milk?

CARLA: Do you like milk?

BRADLEY: No, I hate it!

CARLA: So maybe you spill it on purpose. You just think it's an accident.

BRADLEY: *(Stares angrily down at the table. He feels like she tricked him.)* I don't drink milk. I drink coffee. *(Beat.)* I didn't do anything wrong!

CARLA: Nobody said you did.

BRADLEY: Then how come I have to be here?

CARLA: I was hoping you'd like it here. I was hoping we could be friends. Do you think we can?

BRADLEY: *(Without anger.)* No.

CARLA: Why not?

BRADLEY: *(Matter-of-fact.)* Because I don't like you.

CARLA: I can like you, can't I? You don't have to like me.

(Bradley squirms.)

CARLA: I was hoping you'd be able to teach me some things.

BRADLEY: You're the teacher, not me.

CARLA: That doesn't matter. A teacher can often learn a lot more from a student than a student can learn from a teacher.

BRADLEY: *(Nodding.)* I've taught Mrs. Ebbel a lot.

CARLA: What do you want to teach me?

BRADLEY: What do you want to know?

CARLA: You tell me. What's the most important thing you can teach me?

BRADLEY: *(Ponders a moment.)* The elephant's the biggest animal in the world. But it's afraid of mice.

CARLA: I wonder why that is.

BRADLEY: *(Eagerly.)* Because, if a mouse ran up an elephant's trunk, it would get stuck, and then the elephant wouldn't be able to breathe, and so it would die. That's how most elephants die, you know.

CARLA: I see. Thank you. You're a very good teacher. What else would you like to teach me.

BRADLEY: Nothing. *(Snidely.)* You're not supposed to talk in school.

CARLA: Why not?

BRADLEY: It's a *rule*. Like no sticking gum in the water fountains.

CARLA: Well, in this room, there are no rules. In here, everyone thinks for himself. No one tells you what to do.

BRADLEY: You mean I can stick gum in the water fountain?

CARLA: You could, except I don't have a water fountain.

BRADLEY: Can I break something?

CARLA: Certainly.

BRADLEY: *(Gets up and walks around the room, looking for something to break, then looks back at Carla unsure.)* I'm not in the mood.

CARLA: OK. But if you're ever in the mood, there are lots of things you can break — things I like very much and things other children use.

BRADLEY: I will! *(Sits back down.)* I know karate. *(Raises his hand over the table as if ready to give it a karate chop.)* I can break this table with my bare hand.

CARLA: Ooh. Won't that hurt?

BRADLEY: Nothing ever hurts me. I've broken every table in my house. Call my mother if you don't believe me!

CARLA: I believe you.

BRADLEY: *(Looks at her, surprised that she believes him.)* So now what am I supposed to do?

CARLA: Would you like to draw a picture? I've got a whole box of crayons.

(She gives Bradley a sheet of paper and the box of crayons. Bradley chooses a black crayon and stays with it the whole time.)

BRADLEY: *(While scribbling.)* My parents only feed me dog food.

CARLA: How does it taste?

BRADLEY: *(Stops coloring and looks up at her, surprised by her reaction.)* Delicious! Meaty and sweet.

CARLA: I've always wanted to try it.

BRADLEY: *(After scribbling some more.)* The president called me on the phone last night.

CARLA: How exciting! What'd you talk about.

BRADLEY: *(Still scribbling.)* Hats.

CARLA: What about hats?

BRADLEY: I asked him why he didn't wear a hat like Abraham Lincoln.

CARLA: And what did the president say?

BRADLEY: I'm not allowed to tell you. It's top secret. *(Scribbles some more.)* Done! *(Holds up his picture.)*

CARLA: That's very nice.

BRADLEY: It's a picture of night time.

CARLA: Oh, I thought it was the floor of a barber shop, after someone with black curly hair got his hair cut.

BRADLEY: That's what it is! That's what I meant.

CARLA: It's very good. May I have it?

BRADLEY: *(Suspiciously.)* What for?

CARLA: I'd like to hang it up on my wall.

BRADLEY: *(Stares at her in amazement.)* No, it's mine!

CARLA: I was hoping you'd let me.

BRADLEY: It costs a dollar.

CARLA: I'm sure it's worth it.

(Bradley shakes his head.)

CARLA: OK. But, if you ever change your mind . . .

BRADLEY: You can make me give it to you.

CARLA: No, I can't do that.

BRADLEY: Sure you can! Teachers can make kids do things all the time.

CARLA: Not in here. *(She holds out her hand for him to shake.)* I've enjoyed your visit very much. Thank you for sharing so much with me.

(Bradley, taking his picture, backs away from her without shaking her hand. He walks out of her office, then rips up his picture and drops it on the ground.)

Time on Fire
Timothy Mason

Time on Fire follows the lives of a group of young people in New England during the momentous early years of the American Revolution, 1775 and 1776. Each is caught up in the ensuing turbulence: from indentured servants to landed gentry, from runaway slaves to Quaker pacifists, including a young British spy — no one escapes the combustion of war unscathed or unchanged.

Three Males and One Female

In the first scene, Tribulation, a young Quaker boy, seeks out his sister, Epiphany, for council. In the next scene, a young drummer boy and Winston Onslow, a young teacher who has volunteered to fight for freedom, talk about their families.

Epiphany crosses and sits, and we have moved to the Bradshaw house, later that day. Tribulation enters and sees his sister lost in thought.

TRIBULATION: Epiphany?

EPIPHANY: I think I shall dedicate myself to God. I don't trust anyone else.

TRIBULATION: Epiphany, please, this is important.
(Epiphany looks at her brother, and then decides not to get into it.)

EPIPHANY: Yes, Brother? I'm here.

TRIBULATION: I did the right thing, didn't I?

EPIPHANY: You mean about the man in the barn?

TRIBULATION: Did I do the right thing? I don't know if I did the right thing. And now they're treating me like a hero and I know it should feel good, but it doesn't.

EPIPHANY: I think you need to be still and listen. God will tell you what to do.

TRIBULATION: But it's too late for that, I needed God to tell me what to do this morning! Was God telling me to lock that man in and run for the militia, or was it just me doing it? When I tell myself it was God telling me, I feel I did the right thing. But maybe it just felt . . . adventurous, finding the enemy soldier, to be the one who turned him in. I'm not allowed to go to war, but I was the one who caught the redcoat. That felt good, it still feels good. And it doesn't feel like God.

EPIPHANY: I wish Father were easier to talk to.

TRIBULATION: Father, I tried talking to Father, Father gave me a dollar. You're the one I want to talk to. Sister, the man pounded on the door. He was sound asleep when I found him, I think I got the door shut before he saw my face, I hope so. I hope he didn't see my face, I pray to God he didn't see my face. I hope he thinks it was just some grown-up who caught him. He cried, Epiphany. After I got the door shut and barred, he pounded and he begged me to let him out. I never said a word. And then he started to cry, I could hear him. And I could have done it, I could have opened the door. He promised he would just go away, he wouldn't hurt anyone, he wouldn't set any more fires. He was hurt, he was tired and hungry. I could have lifted the bar and run. Nobody would have known. He could have walked out the door and into the woods. I could have had mercy on him, Epiphany, and I didn't.

(They're silent for a moment.)

TRIBULATION: *(Continuing.)* It's time to go to Meeting.

EPIPHANY: If you had opened that door he might have walked into the woods and traveled back to his comrades in arms. I suppose he might have starved to death in the forest. He might have come out of the barn with a pistol and done you great harm, Brother, we don't know. Perhaps in some way we can't understand, you were for that soldier an instrument of God's grace.

(Tribulation starts off.)

TRIBULATION: Epiphany, they're going to hang him.

(Epiphany follows him off.)

EPIPHANY: The Bible says it is through tribulation we must enter the Kingdom of God.

TRIBULATION: Well I hope the Bible doesn't mean me.

(Epiphany and Tribulation exit.)

+ + +

The Drummer claps his hands and stamps a foot in time to a country tune of the period. Winston reclines at the Drummer's feet, enjoying the music. They're lit by the flickering glow of a campfire. The offstage Fiddler finishes.

DRUMMER: The da used to play that one on fiddle.

WINSTON: It's very lively, is it Irish?

(The Drummer doesn't know what he means.)

DRUMMER: It's music. On fiddle.

WINSTON: Yes, thank you. Lovely.

DRUMMER: The da played fiddle just fine.

WINSTON: I'm sure he did.

DRUMMER: Known for it.

WINSTON: Oh, yes?

DRUMMER: People came to hear him. Filled the house.

WINSTON: You know I don't believe I've ever heard you talk

about your family. And now, knowing you, you won't say another word.

(Winston waits.)

WINSTON: *(Continuing.)* You won't even tell me your Christian name.

DRUMMER: I'm Drummer.

WINSTON: Yes, of course. All right. My mother is French, my father is English, he's a vicar. You know what a vicar is, a priest? Father is vicar at the parish church of St. Cross in Oxford. They live in Holywell Street. That's where I lived until I was about your age, in a pale green house in Holywell Street. Are you ready for sleep, now, Drummer?

DRUMMER: I'm awake.

WINSTON: When I was your age Father packed us all up, me and my sister and mother, and moved us to New London in Connecticut. He'd been called, you see, to start a parish in the new world, by God he'd been called. But then my sister died and my mother became ill and they went back to the pale green house in Holywell Street and I stayed on for the opportunities. And there you have it.

DRUMMER: Why did your sister die?

WINSTON: I don't know why she died. Do you mean what did she die of? It was the smallpox carried her off. Her name was Jeannette, she was two years older. When she was sick I remember thinking we could save her if we could just get her back to Holywell Street. Because the name, "Holywell," it's pronounced "Holly" but it used to mean "holy." And the legend was that on the site of our little street in Oxford was a holy well where an ancient people held pagan rites, where people came to be healed by the waters of the holy well. I was a child.

DRUMMER: My dad and his two mates played on fiddle. They was all right.

WINSTON: I'm sure they were.

DRUMMER: You weren't there.

WINSTON: No, no, I wasn't, I just assume from what you say that . . .

DRUMMER: They filled the house.

WINSTON: Yes.

DRUMMER: Some of my sisters would dance sometimes, and sometimes even Ma.

WINSTON: It sounds grand.

DRUMMER: They all got the front end of their heads cut off, the top of their heads. The da and me ma and all the rest on em.

WINSTON: Good God.

DRUMMER: Injuns came at us in middle of night, we was all sleepin. Narragansetts. We knew 'em, the da knew 'em. I knew em. Friends, in a way, almost. The da traded with 'em. I knew some of the boys, they'd come, we'd play when the grown-ups traded. They didn't leave no one alive in the house cept me, and that's only cause they never found me. I can be invisible, so I made myself invisible and just lay there and they couldn't find me. I thought I should do something but I couldn't do anything, there were too many of them and they were bigger than me. So I just lay there. I wish I done something but I didn't. I'm very sorry

WINSTON: How old were you?

DRUMMER: Twelve or so.

WINSTON: This year? All this happened this year?

DRUMMER: Redcoats paid the Injuns to do it.

WINSTON: What do you mean?

DRUMMER: They give the Narragansetts guns and hatchets and said wipe em out, we'll give you money and land.

WINSTON: Why do you say that, what makes you think . . .

DRUMMER: Cause that's what happened. Wiped out the whole village almost. Then I went in to Boston cause I needed to eat.

WINSTON: Surely not. I mean, perhaps that's how it seemed to you, you were confused and frightened and looking for some sort of explanation for this horror, anything to make sense of something so senseless . . .

DRUMMER: Why do you talk so much? You weren't there.

WINSTON: The British are our opponents in war, a violent, terrible war, you and I both know what it can be like. But they're not savages, for God's sake.

DRUMMER: I was invisible, I watched it. Redcoats were there, two of em, they said here's one, here's another one, this one here's still alive. They couldn't see me, I had a red cloak all over me, I was invisible.

(The two of them are silent, each with his own thoughts. Offstage the Fiddler strikes up a tune.)

WINSTON: When this is over, when our part in this is over, I want you to come home with me. To Connecticut. We'll make a home. I'll find a wife. You can be our son. Drummer?

DRUMMER: I'm awake.

(The campfire flickers out.)

Monologues

Anne of Green Gables

R. N. Sandberg (adapted from
L. M. Montgomery

Anne of Green Gables is a faithful adaptation of L. M. Montgomery's classic tale of the same name. Telling the story of Anne, the high-spirited little girl who captures the hearts of everyone in the quaint village of Avonlea, this plays unlocks the hearts of all.

Female

In the speech below, Anne tells Marilla, the woman who has been caring for her temporarily, about the circumstances of her life.

ANNE: *(Softly, to herself.)* I'm not going to think about going back. I'm going to enjoy my breakfast and these trees and oh, look, there's one little early rose out! Isn't pink the most bewitching color in the entire world? I love it, but I can't wear it. Redheaded people can't wear pink not even in imagination. Did you ever know of anybody whose hair was red when she was young, but got to be another color when she grew up?

[MARILLA: No, I don't know as I ever did, and I shouldn't think it likely to happen in your case, either.]

ANNE: Well, there's another hope gone. My life is a perfect graveyard of buried hopes. That's a sentence I read in a book once. I say it to comfort myself whenever I'm disappointed in anything. It's so nice and romantic, don't you think.

[MARILLA: Since you're bent on talking, you might as well talk to some purpose. Tell me what you know about yourself. Where were you born and such?]

ANNE: [Bollingbroke, Nova Scotia.] My father was Walter Shirley, and he was a teacher in the high school. My mother was Bertha Shirley. Aren't Walter and Bertha lovely names?

[MARILLA: A person's name doesn't matter as long as she behaves herself.]

ANNE: *(She talks matter-of-factly as she eats.)* My mother was a teacher, too, but Mrs. Thomas said they were a pair of babies and poor as church mice. They went to live in a teeny-weeny, little yellow house. I never really saw it, but I've imagined it thousands of times. Honeysuckle over the parlor window, lilacs in the —

[MARILLA: I don't need your imaginings. Stick to the bald facts.]

ANNE: Mrs. Thomas said I was the homeliest baby she ever saw, nothing but eyes. But my mother thought I was perfectly beautiful. I'm glad she was satisfied with me, because she didn't live long, you see. She died of fever when I was just three months old. My father died four days after. There was no family to take me in, and nobody wanted me. But finally, Mrs. Thomas took me, even though she had a drunken husband. I lived with them until I was eight. I helped look after their children — there were four of them younger than me. Then Mr. Thomas was killed falling under a train, and his mother offered to take Mrs. Thomas and the children, but she didn't want me. Finally Mrs. Hammond took me since I was handy with children. She had two when I came, and afterwards twins three times in succession. When Mr. Hammond died, she broke up housekeeping, divided her children among her relatives, and went to the States. I had to go to the asylum because nobody would take me. I was there four months. And then, Mrs. Blewett came. Those are the facts. *(Silence for a moment.)*

The Boy Who Talked to Whales
Webster Smalley

Set near Puget Sound in the Northwest, Jerry befriends and learns to communicate with Ooka, a fifty-foot whale that has escaped from whalers. Together with his friend, Meg, Jerry devises a plan to help Ooka protect herself, but, in the process, they create an international crisis that they have to help the president of the United States resolve.

Male

Jerry suddenly seizes the opportunity to tell millions of other kids on television why he wants to save Ooka.

JERRY: About Ooka? *(Looks at camera. A thought.)* Are there kids out there?
(McLean nods. Jerry looks at the invisible cameras. A light: the children will hear him. This is an outpouring of feelings, not a calculated speech.)
You kids have to know how I feel. Ooka is the most wonderful animal in the world. I've had lots of animals as pets — great animals — a cat, mice, even spiders — I loved 'em all. I had a dog once, and it got hit by a car. I don't ever want another dog, 'cause I don't want to see a dog I love die like that. Ooka is the most lovely, beautiful animal in the world, but she doesn't understand people — the way we are. She hasn't done anything so she should be hurt — or killed.
(McLean prevents Rock from interrupting.)

Don't let Mr. O'Connell or Commander Rock do anything to her. Ooka is a helpless animal, like a dog in front of a car. She doesn't understand people, but she trusts me. Like my dog did. I don't know if the grown-ups understand, but I sure hope you kids do. So help me! Save Ooka. Tell everybody. Do something — telephone, write letters, shout — run down the street and yell it. I don't know who to ask — ask everyone. The television, newspapers, the Navy, the world! Save Ooka! Help me!

(Jerry is exhausted. McLean quickly takes over before Rock or O'Connell have time to speak.)

Doors
Suzan L. Zeder

Doors examines the impact of divorce and separation in the lives of young people. Seen through the eyes of eleven-year-old Jeff, the play mixes realism and fantasy as the day his parents decide to get a divorce painfully unfolds.

Male

Distracted and upset by the sounds of his parents arguing, Jeff attempts to concentrate on building a model.

✢ ✢ ✢

At rise, Jeff is alone on stage, seated at the desk. He is working intently on a large, complicated model of a spaceship. The model is almost finished. Jeff works with great concentration with the directions and a tube of glue.

The first sounds we hear are muffled voices coming from Jeff's parents' room. They are arguing. This argument will be ongoing during most of the play; at times, specific voices and words will be heard, at other times, muffled sound, sometimes, nothing. Care should be taken to preserve the illusion that the argument is continuous without detracting from the primary focus, which is to be on stage with Jeff and his actions.

Jeff tries to concentrate on his task of building the model, but he is obviously distracted and upset by the sounds coming from behind the door. He reads from the directions.

JEFF: "When the glue is partially set, insert cockpit window flaps G and H into the main body of the craft." *(The sounds of the argument grow louder and Jeff tries to concentrate harder.)* "Hold firmly in place for a few seconds until the glue sets . . ." *(There is another sound from behind the door. Jeff looks up, the part slips. He tries again.)* "When the glue is partially set, insert cockpit window flaps G and H into the main body of the craft." *(As Jeff lines up parts, a series of angry bursts are heard, they register on his face, but he does not move.)* . . . "until the glue sets" . . . *(Jeff rises, turns on the stereo set, and returns to the model.)* "Insert wheel hub N into wheel rim O and affix the wheel assembly to landing gear C." *(He looks all over the model.)* Where's the landing gear? Where's the landing gear? Where's that . . . *(Sounds from behind the door increase. Jeff picks up the model, looking for the landing gear and the cockpit falls off. The phone rings. Jeff looks at the door. The phone rings again. Jeff tries to return to the model, the phone rings again.)* "Insert wheel hub" . . . yeah . . . yeah . . . yeah . . . "affix to landing GEAR!" *(The phone continues to ring. Finally, Jeff rises and answers. The stereo is very loud.)* Hello? Just a second. *(Jeff puts down the phone, crosses to the stereo, and turns it off. He returns to the phone.)* Sorry. Hello, Gramma. Yeah, this is Jeff. Yeah, we got out of school last week . . . No, I'm not going to camp this year . . . Gramma, they don't have camps for grandmothers. *(Sounds behind the door increase.)* Yeah, they're both here, but they can't come to the phone right now. They're in their room with the door closed, and I don't think I'd better . . . I'll tell them you called. I'm sure Mom will call you back later . . . Yeah, you too, Gramma. Bye. *(Jeff hangs up the phone, and crosses back to the desk, on the way he turns on the stereo and the TV very loud.)* Stop it. Stop it! STOP IT! *(Jeff sits and buries his face in his hands.)*

Don't Eat Little Charlie
Tankred Dorst with Ursula Ehler,
translated by Ella Wildridge

Magical and surreal, *Don't Eat Little Charlie* is a fairytale
whose title character, Charlie, doesn't seem to grow. And what's
worse, his brother Olmo, who can eat anything, wants to eat
him. The colorful Pug, who also lives with Charlie and his
brother in Granmaha's frenzied house, tricks Olmo into leaving so he can't eat any of them. But once outside Olmo gets so
big eating other things he can't get back in until he breaks
through the wall. Now the landlord's upset. In the end, the only
path to survival is through the magic and music of Antunes O
Rei, the Brazilian music king, who returns to claim his crown
from Granmaha.

Male

In the following speech, Charlie's friend, Pug, admits that lots
of people find him funny to look at — but why?

✦ ✦ ✦

PUG: Lots of people do find me funny. But why? *(Hurt.)* I've
    scrutinized myself in the mirror to see what effect my
    appearance has. I didn't find anything to laugh about. So
    why do people laugh? I've sat at the knees of important peo-
    ple. In my younger years I was chauffeur-driven from
    Geneva to Paris, many, many times. I spent elegant weeks
    in the Ritz Hotel. I've seen important monuments and his-
    toric sites. Those smells. How different the Boulevard des
    Anglais is from the corner of Rue St. Honoré at the Lou-

vre. How exciting the trail of smells left by the dukes' Great Danes at the Place d'Etoile. The iron lamp posts I used to sniff along, post by post — and the plinths.

That, you fizzing sparkler, is all a question of lifestyle. And so it might have gone on. But after the great stock-market crash, they had to dispose of me. I am an object of value, you know — not just anyone can afford to buy me. So I went to the coloratura soprano. Distinct possibilities, I thought at the start. Interesting. How does singing work, I wondered. To sing is to breathe. You breathe not only from the thorax, you breathe right from your buttocks. Breathing — it's like a column inside your body. And up on top of this column notes can balance, like little balls on the jets of a fountain. Very interesting.

The whole milieu — highly interesting. The atmosphere of the theater! Dressing room! Makeup! First-night fever! An artist of note. But unfortunately the relationship turned out to be too full of stress. She couldn't endure my snoring, nor I the hours and hours of her warm-up before every performance. I had to yowl along whether I wanted to or not. And so we decided to part. It was all downhill from then on. The boredom of middle-class family life. Finally — to cut a long story short, I was abandoned by an au-pair at the station buffet.

Hula Heart
Velina Hasu Houston

Seven-year-old Sean "Kilo" Hauptmann, a multiethnic boy from Hawaii, moves to Southern California with his family, where he attempts to pursue his love of the hula. Sean befriends Caleb, another boy who shares like traditions, but most of his new mainland acquaintances mock them. In the clash of pop culture and native traditions, Sean learns much about himself and his place in life.

Male

In the speech below, Sean reflects on his life in the Hawaiian Islands and wonders if he'll ever fit into his new life on the mainland.

✦ ✦ ✦

Sean Hauptmann enters a nondescript, twilight stage space carrying a blanket and pillow. He rubs his eyes and looks up at the stars, then out at the audience.

SEAN: When I lived in Honolulu in Kaimuki, I looked at the stars all the time. Maybe because it was what my Hawaiian name was all about — Kilohoku, star gazer. Maybe because they were there, big and milky white like a thousand more islands connected to all of Hawaii. Then my dad died, and I kind of thought that he became one of those stars, that the angels made him into a star so that I could always see him. *(Looks up at the sky and waves.)* Hi, Dad! *(Punches pillow to make it soft, tries to get comfortable to sleep, but cannot.)*

Mom wants to be closer to her sister since Dad's gone. But since we moved to Manhattan Beach, I don't sleep so good. Bad dreams! It's beautiful and all, just like Hawaii, but — get this! — kids think I'm *haole!* Believe it, yeah. I know I don't look like King Kamehameha. That's 'cause I got plenty kind of races. I'm chop suey! *(Quick pause.)* Now, I'm living on a humongous island called the mainland, and it's a cool enough place all right, but am I ever going to fit in?

The Invisible Man
Len Jenkins

Adapted from the H. G. Wells story and set in the 1950s, Jack Griffin — face bandaged — is living in an old motel near a nuclear power plant. He befriends Jim, a small boy, whose father has been the caretaker of the plant until his recent death. In the course of serving as the boy's father figure, Jack reveals the reason he must wear bandages is because a nuclear accident at the plant caused him to become invisible. But is this the truth? In the process of answering this question, Jim is forced to make difficult decisions.

Male

In the opening speech of *The Invisible Man,* Jim, who has been watching a movie at the drive-in, comes forward to set the scene and his place in it. In the next speech, the invisible man, Jack Griffith, explains to Jim how he became invisible.

✦ ✦ ✦

Winter 1957. Stardust Drive-In Movie Theater. Playground and small stage below screen. Sound of cars pulling in, their headlight beams swinging across screen as audience is being seated. Sky darkens, and Jim sneaks into his spot to watch movie. Houselights out. Projector flickers, and Movietone News rolls. (Suggested contents of news: "Home of the future! Amazing new appliances!" "Dr. Cosmo Gibson tours Glowville Nuclear Facility." or "Dr. Cosmo Gibson testifies in Washington before the President's Atomic Energy Commission." "Poodle skirts are in!" etc.) Jim watches newsreel. Movietone News ends. Screen fills with illustrated freeze-frame: "Our Popcorn Is Dee-licious." Jim comes downstage, eating from bag of popcorn.

JIM: Everything's half price at the Snack Shack tonight. Last night of the season. I got a large — with extra butter. You see that newsreel? The future is gonna be amazing. And since I'm only a kid, I get to live in it. Let's see, this is 1957. I should be around in the year 2000, flying everywhere with a rocket on my back!

You know what I think? Someday there's gonna be people on the moon. And on the planet Mars. My dad believed that, and he was an engineer. He was really smart. He once told me that . . .

Anyway, he got killed in Korea. Fighting the Chinese communists. My mom says that war was stupid, and the whole damn country of Korea wasn't worth my dad's life. That was a few years ago. Since then it's been just Mom and me.

The world may be exciting these days, but we're pretty much out of it around here, especially at the Sleep Daze Inn. That's the hotel my mom runs, right up the road. Nobody comes in the fall and winter, but we stay open anyway. Mom's always hoping we'll get lucky. Too bad tonight's the last night. Winter's coming.

✦ ✦ ✦

GRIFFIN: There are no miracles, Jim. Think. Most of the human body — or this table for that matter — *(Hits table with invisible hand.)* is actually empty space. But the tiny particles that are there, the atoms, are arranged so they reflect light and make us visible. If you change the arrangement of those atoms, so they let the light just pass right through — abracadabra. You're invisible.

No fantasy, Jim. Plutonium is a new element that can be a much greater power source than uranium. I was working on a plutonium fusion technique at Glowville. The experiments needed huge amounts of power and high levels of radiation.

One night I was working with this photon accelerator chamber. I wasn't wearing lead shields — too clumsy. I accidentally stepped in front of the beta beam. I thought nothing of it, finished my work, and went home.

Later that night, my hands went first. They became like clouded glass, and then clearer and clearer. My whole body became glassy, the bones and arteries faded, vanished, and the little white nerves went last. The final thing was my shadow on the floor there until almost the end. Light could find something, even if the human eye could not — and then even my shadow was gone.

It lasted only a few months, and I gradually reappeared. One night, I broke in and exposed myself to the reactor's radiation levels again. Again, poof! I disappeared. In my lab I've been trying to perfect a radiation technique that works without the reactor's enormous power. No success as yet.

Kindertransport
Diane Samuels

Moving simultaneously back and forth through time, *Kindertransport* depicts the parallel lives of Evelyn and her daughter, Faith, in the present, and Eva (Evelyn's younger self) and her mother, Helga, in the past, as they prepare for separation. Evelyn prepares Faith to go out into the world and establish her own life, as Helga prepares Eva for the uncertainty of a world at war.

Female

Here Little Eva crosses the border out of Nazi Germany during the kindertransport, then to Holland and England and safety.

✦ ✦ ✦

Sounds of a train speeding along. Children's excited chatter. In German, "The border, the border, the border."

EVA: It is the border! The border! Can't get us now! We're out! Out! Stuff your stupid Hitler. Stuff your stupid toffees! *(She throws down the toffee.)* Keep them! Hope your eyes fall out and you die the worst death on earth! Hope you all rot in hell forever and ever! Hope no one buries you! Hope the rats come and eat up all your remains until there's nothing left! *(Sounds of a train stopping. Sounds of a buzzing, busy, happy crowd at a railway station. A voice saying in Dutch: "Have as many sweets and as much lemonade as you want.")*

(Greedily eating and drinking.) You know what? That Dutch lady said we can have as many cakes as we want. And sweets. And lemonade. I'm going to stuff my pockets for later. Who says it's naughty? They all want us to be happy, don't they? Well, that's what I'm doing. Making myself happy.

(Sound of a ship's horn and the lapping of waves. Tired, muted children's chatter.)

You know what? If you lick your lips you'll taste the salt. Sea salt. What d'you mean, Hook of Holland? It can't be. It's nothing like one. It isn't. Look at it. How's that a hook? *(Coughing.)* Excuse me . . . *(About to vomit.)* . . . it won't come . . . No, I'm fine . . . Really . . . It's just nothing . . . Nothing will come out of me.

(Sound of a ship's horn.)

This is Harwich, you know. It really is England.

(Sounds of disembarkation. Children's chatter and adult English voices, "Come along now," "Keep moving," "Move to the right, please.")

Can you just go through like that? Don't they search you? *(Eva stops and bends down suddenly. Picking up one penny.)* A penny. They have big money here. It must be a sign of good luck.

(Eva pockets the penny.)

Time on Fire
Timothy Mason

Time on Fire follows the lives of a group of young people in New England during the momentous early years of the American Revolution, 1775 and 1776. Each is caught up in the ensuing turbulence: from indentured servants to landed gentry, from runaway slaves to Quaker pacifists, including a young British spy — no one escapes the combustion of war unscathed or unchanged.

Male

Tribulation, a young Quaker boy, has caught a British spy who was responsible for blowing up his father's mill. Wounded and having narrowly escaped after the explosion, the British officer has been hiding in the neighbor's barn. The locals have declared Tribulation a hero for his noble act, but he feels responsible for this young man's death — as he will certainly hang for his sabotage. Here Tribulation seeks the counsel of his sister, Epiphany.

✤ ✤ ✤

TRIBULATION: Did I do the right thing? I don't know if I did the right thing. And now they're treating me like a hero and I know it should feel good, but it doesn't. Was God telling me to lock that man in and run for the militia, or was it just me doing it? When I tell myself it was God telling me, I feel I did the right thing. But maybe it just felt . . . adventurous, finding the enemy soldier, to be the one who turned him in. I'm not allowed to go to war, but I was the one who caught the redcoat. That felt good, it still feels good. And it doesn't feel like God.

Sister, the man pounded on the door. He was sound asleep when I found him, I think I got the door shut before he saw my face, I hope so. I hope he didn't see my face, I pray to God he didn't see my face. I hope he thinks it was just some grown-up who caught him. He cried, Epiphany. After I got the door shut and barred, he pounded and he begged me to let him out. I never said a word. And then he started to cry, I could hear him. And I could have done it, I could have opened the door. He promised he would just go away, he wouldn't hurt anyone, he wouldn't set any more fires. He was hurt, he was tired and hungry. I could have lifted the bar and run. Nobody would have known. He could have walked out the door and into the woods. I could have had mercy on him, Epiphany, and I didn't.

Permission Acknowledgments

The Adventures of Huckleberry Finn by Timothy Mason. © 2001 by Timothy Mason. Reprinted by permission of the author. All inquiries should be addressed to Mitch Douglas, ICM, 40 West 57th Street, New York, NY 10019.

Afternoon of the Elves by Y York. © 2000 by Y. York. All rights reserved. From the book by Janet Taylor Lisle. All inquiries regarding performance rights should be addressed to Dramatic Publishing, 311 Washington Street, Woodstock, IL 60098. Tel: (810) 338-8981.

Anne of Green Gables by R. N. Sandberg. © 2001 by R. N. Sandberg. Reprinted by permission of Anchorage Press Plays. All inquiries should be addressed to Anchorage Press Plays, International Agency of Plays for Young People, PO Box 2901, Louisville, KY 40201. Tel: (502) 583-2288; fax: (502) 583-2281; e-mail: applays@bellsouth.net.

Beauty and the Beast by Constance Congdon. © 2002 by Constance Congdon. Reprinted by permission of The Children's Theatre Company. All inquiries should be addressed to Script Licensing Dept., The Children's Theater Co., 2400 Third Avenue South, Minneapolis, MN 55404.

The Boy Who Stole the Stars by Julian Wiles. © 1985 by Julian Wiles. All rights reserved (*The Boy Who Stole the Stars*). All inquiries regarding performance rights should be addressed to Dramatic Publishing, 311 Washington Street, Woodstock, IL 60098. Tel: (810) 338-8981.

The Boy Who Talked to Whales by Webster Smalley. © 1981 by Webster Smalley. Reprinted by permission of Anchorage Press Plays. All inquiries should be addressed to Marilee Miller, Anchorage Press Plays, International Agency of Plays for Young People, PO Box 2901, Louisville, KY 40201. Tel: (502) 583-2288; fax: (502) 583-2281; e-mail: applays@bellsouth.net.

Dogbrain by Michael Weller. © 2002 by Michael Weller. Reprinted by permission of the author. All inquires should be addressed to